Read and share this book in the best of
health!

Happy New Year!

♡ Marla

The Physiology Storybook
An owner's manual for the human body
2nd Edition

Marla Richmond, M.S.

Joie Publications

Manufactured in the United States of America
Library of Congress Control Number: 2006920165
ISBN: 9780967441023

Conceptual Illustrator: Marla Richmond
Graphic Illustrator: Karen Hakimian, Crea.tif ink
Editor: Fran S. Sherman
Book Consultation: Tabby House
Back Cover Photo by: Larry Rappaport

Joie Publications
P.O. Box 1204
Northbrook, IL 60065

Dedication

The first edition of *The Physiology Storybook: An Owner's Manual for the Human Body* was dedicated to my father and mentor, who passed away before its 2000 publication. Fortunately, he was able to read it and beam with pride (and of course take credit) for his daughter's gifts in its creation. *The Physiology Storybook, 2nd edition*, is dedicated to my children, Matthew and Melanie, the greatest pride of my life. May they use their own gifts and tenacity to help heal the world one day at a time, one person at a time.

Acknowledgments

Many thanks to all of the individuals who participated in and supported this project.

Thank you, Michael, for again making this possible. And thank you too for making this work a gift to those who otherwise may never have seen it.

Matthew, thank you for translating this wonderful book into Spanish. I look forward to its future publication.

To Karen, my graphic artist, and Fran, my editor, who were once again forced to learn and review exercise and nutrition science.

Thank you, Karen, for meeting and exceeding the incredible demands of updating and rewriting the chapters of this book. You were brilliantly able to reproduce and improve all of my original pencil drawings.

Thank you, Fran, for your friendship, love, continued dedication and incomparable work in the masterful editing of the second edition.

My humblest gratitude to all of the reviewers.

Peter K. Healey, Ph.D., Professor of Physiology and retired Director of Graduate Programs in Exercise Physiology, Benedictine University, Lisle, Illinois

Alfred, "Roc" Ordman, Ph.D., Chair and Professor of Biochemistry, Beloit College, Beloit, Wisconsin

Michael DiMuzio, Ph.D., Associate Professor, Northwestern University, Director of the North Shore Osteoporosis Clinic, Deerfield, Illinois

Steven Blair, Ph.D., President and C.E.O. of Cooper Institute, Dallas, Texas

Wayne Westcott, Ph.D., Research Director of the South Shore YMCA and author of twenty fitness books

Cedric X. Bryant, Ph.D., FACSM Chief Exercise Physiologist/Vice President of Educational Services, American Council on Exercise

Mary E. Sanders, Ph.D., Associate Professor, School of Medicine, University of Nevada, Reno, Nevada

Nancy Tierney, M.S., Director of Fitness/Wellness, Northwestern University, Evanston, Illinois

Victoria Long, M.A., retired Physical and Health Educator/Staff Wellness Director, Glenbrook North High School, Northbrook, Illinois

Many thanks to my research assistant, Irene, and my personal assistant, Rita, for holding me up every week, no matter how heavy things got.

Thank you to the angels recently sent to me for love, support, and most of all, hope for the future.

And last but not least—thank you a million times to my "girls," a sisterhood of women who have blessed me with their presence every day of my professional life—without them I could not live my life as joyously.

Foreword

You are about to enter a fascinating world—the world about *you*. A human being is probably the most complex structure ever developed. The human body is far more sophisticated than the best computer, more reliable than most machines, and more adaptable to changing conditions than the best temperature control systems. Many machines come with instruction manuals and maintenance schedules. If you wish to have your car perform optimally, for example, you read the manual and follow the suggestions given.

Both you and your automobile are complex machines. The better you understand them, the better both will serve you. Automobile manufacturers will tell you that they are not responsible for the functioning of your vehicle if you do not follow suggested maintenance procedures. In a similar manner, you are responsible for the understanding and maintenance of your body. You cannot say that you got a lemon when your body does not function properly if you have not followed proper maintenance procedures.

The Physiology Storybook introduces you to the functioning of the human body in a unique and entertaining way. The study of the human body is fascinating for several reasons: first, the way the body works is very logical; second, the more we know about the body's functioning, the more we are able to see the body as an integrated unit, not just a series of individual and separate systems; and third, you are studying about *you*, your own machine, with all of its beautifully engineered parts working together. In addition to information about your body's functioning, this book provides you with practical applications and recommendations.

Think of *The Physiology Storybook* as an owner's manual for the human body. You have the responsibility to keep your machine in optimal condition if you want to get the most mileage out of it.

We hope that you enjoy the creative and exciting presentation of anatomical and physiological information in this book. We hope you use the book to develop a better understanding of how you function, and we hope this knowledge will enhance your life.

—*Peter K. Healey, Ph.D.*
Professor of Physiology
Benedictine University

Contents

Contents

Introduction

This is the second edition of *The Physiology Storybook: An Owner's Manual for the Human Body*. If you read the first edition, you know that learning the physiology of exercise and nutrition can be clear, understandable, and even exciting!

Physiology is the study of body cells—what they do and how they do it. Body cells make up tissues, tissues form organs, and organs work together as body systems. Everything that happens during the course of a day presents our cells with a variety of experiences. With each event, a new story unfolds . . . a story about how cells, tissues, organs, and systems work together to adapt and maintain balance. *The Physiology Storybook* illustrates and interprets the stories in an entertaining and memorable way.

While chemical messengers do not typically travel on wave runners and nutrients do not use a diving board to enter your blood, the body's cells really do monitor their needs and demand that you meet them. If you don't, you will not feel or be well.

Since the publication of *The Physiology Storybook: An Owner's Manual for the Human Body* in 2000, you may have grown and changed a great deal. So has the study of exercise and nutrition science. New research and statistics have made it necessary to modify nutrition and physical activity guidelines. Parameters have been changed for early diagnosis, intervention, and prevention rather than simply the treatment of such diseases as type 2 diabetes, atherosclerosis, high blood pressure, and osteoporosis. Phyl and Phyllis' Physiology Phorums have been rewritten and updated to reflect and include the new information as well as provide you with practical advice and activities.

Your muscle cells will always demand that your heart pump blood to them as fast as they move. The number of calories you use in a day will always be a result of how much you move and what you eat. Still, your body cells are ever-growing and changing. Your understanding of how they work through reading *The Physiology Storybook, An Owner's Manual for the Human Body* will continue to grow and change as well. For each time you open it and look at one of its pages, you will surely discover new details and a new story.

The Body's Systems

Chapter 1
The Nervous System

The Human Nervous System

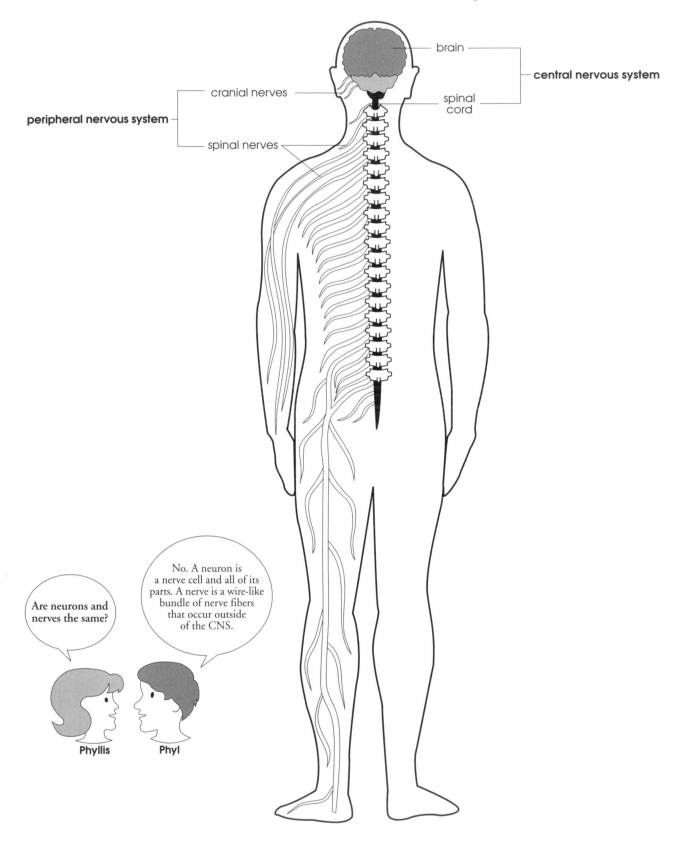

The human nervous system is made up of the central nervous system (CNS), which consists of the brain and the spinal cord, and the peripheral nervous system (PNS), which is made up of the spinal and cranial nerves.

The Control Center

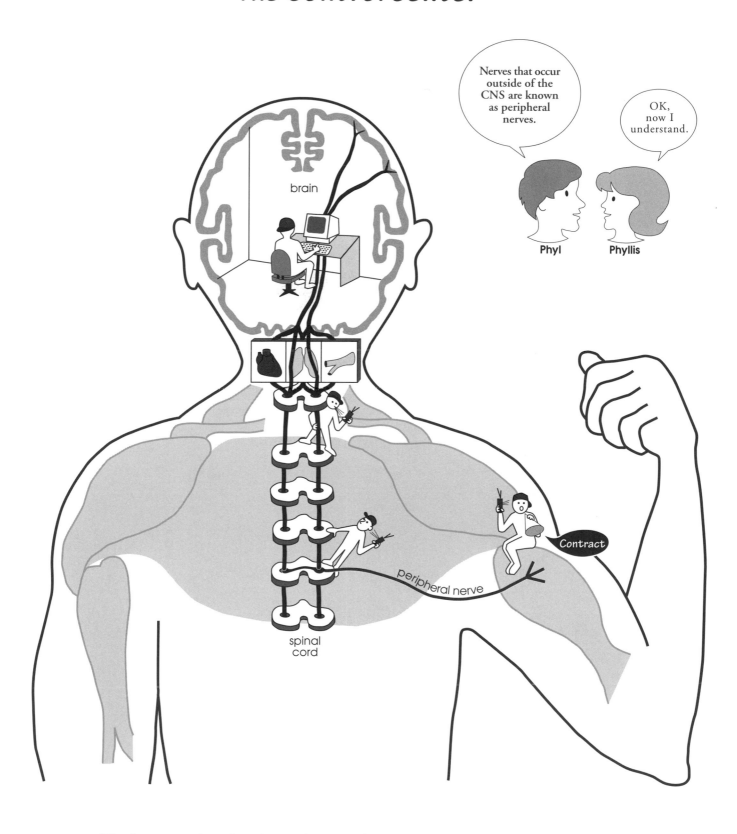

The brain may be referred to as the control center. It sends messages through the spinal cord and out to tissues using a wiring system of nerves that communicate to and from all of the body's tissues and organs. The wiring system is called the peripheral nervous system (PNS).

The PNS:
Voluntary and Involuntary Nerves

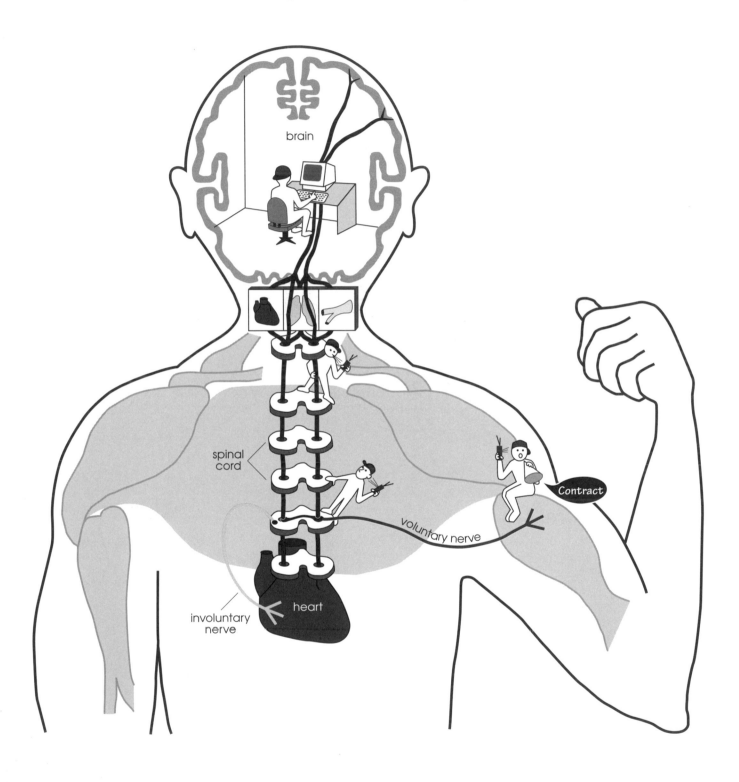

Messages from the CNS travel along the PNS wires. Some messages are voluntary, meaning that we can control them. Some messages are involuntary, meaning that we cannot control them.

Efferent Nerves:
Somatic and Autonomic

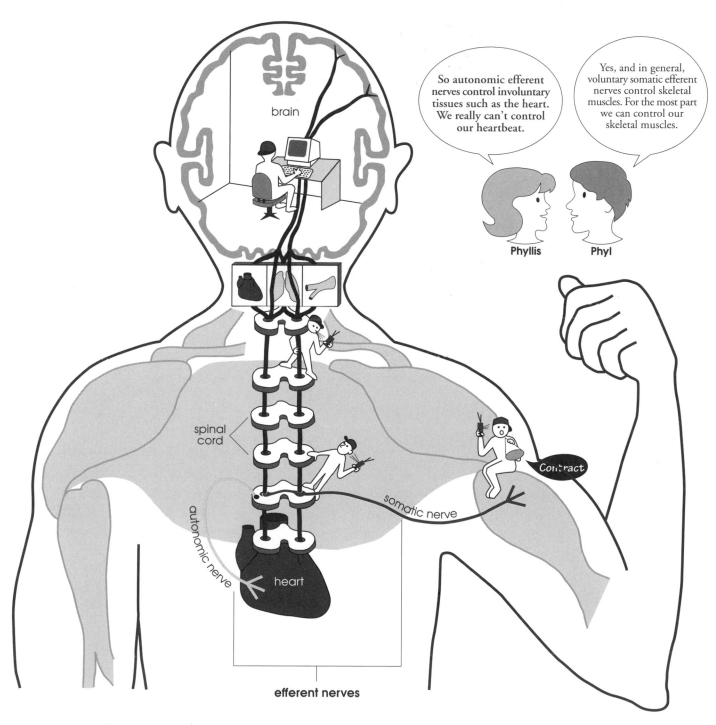

The wires of the PNS that carry messages out to the body's tissues and organs are called efferent nerves. Our efferent nervous system is comprised of two systems: the somatic nervous system and the autonomic nervous system.

Wires that carry messages to skeletal muscles and create movement are called somatic efferent nerves. Some examples of autonomic efferent nerves are those that carry messages to our gastrointestinal tract to promote digestion of food, to our sweat glands to initiate sweating, or to our heart muscle to increase force and rate of pumping.

Afferent Nerves

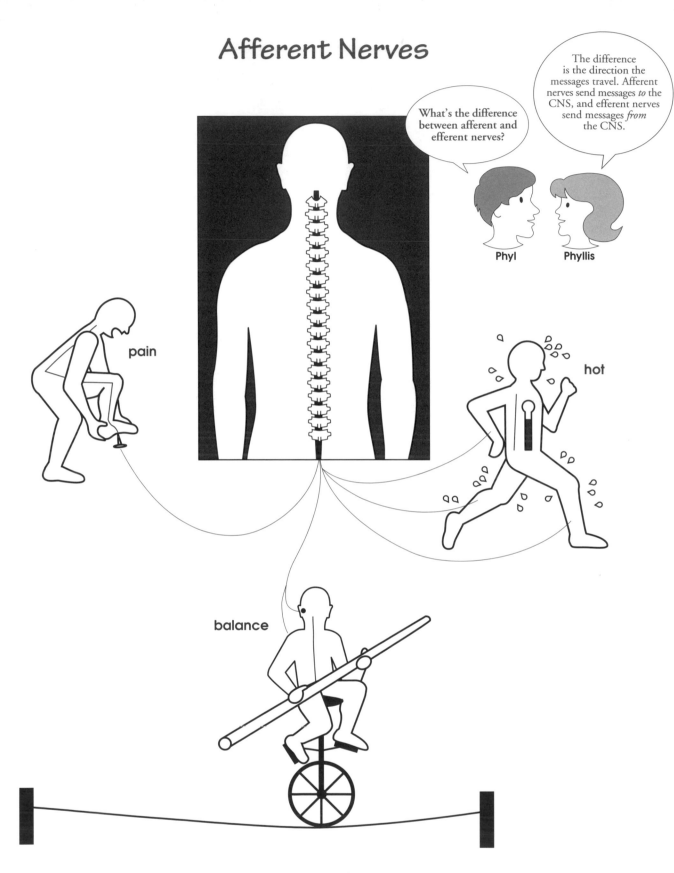

Messages from all over the body are sent back to the CNS along a wiring system of nerves called afferent nerves. These messages tell the brain about all of the events that are taking place in the body. Afferent nerves communicate that the body is hot or cold, or that the body is in pain. These nerves also notify the CNS that we are moving and communicate our position in space.

The Body's Systems

Chapter 2
The Skeletal and Muscular
Systems

The Skeletal System

Phyllis

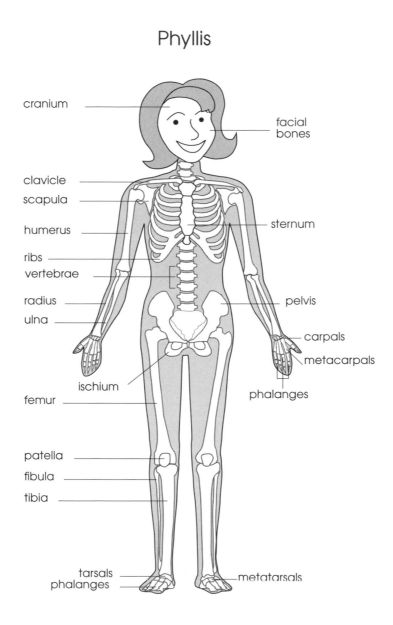

cranium

facial bones

clavicle

scapula

humerus

sternum

ribs

vertebrae

radius

pelvis

ulna

carpals

metacarpals

ischium

phalanges

femur

patella

fibula

tibia

tarsals
phalanges

metatarsals

The skeletal system is made up of bones. Bones create the framework for the body. They also house and protect our organs, the brain and the spinal cord, and the heart and lungs. Bones serve as a mineral reservoir and they contain bone marrow, where all of the blood cells of the body are made.

The Muscular System

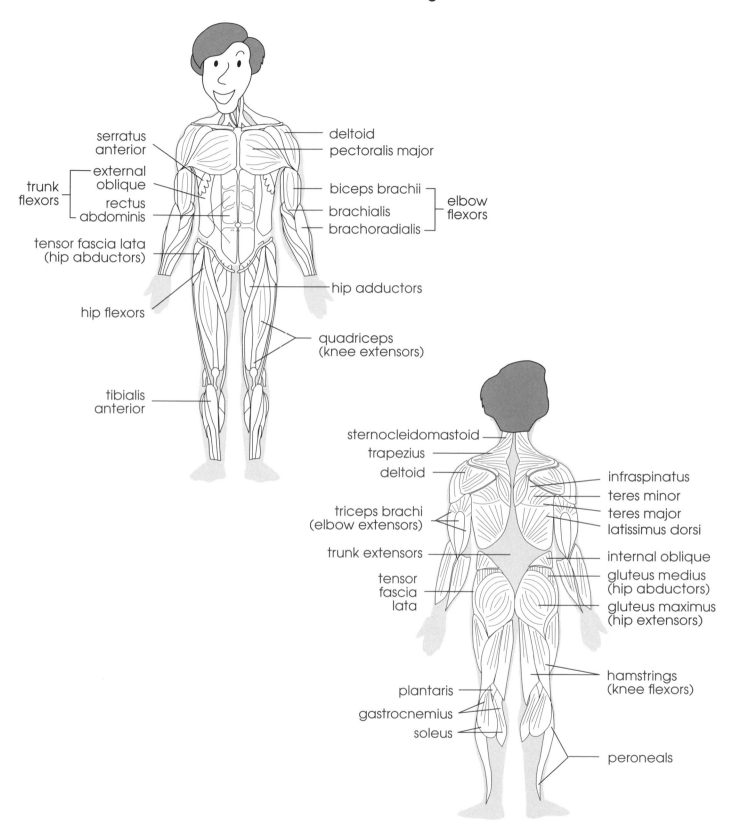

serratus anterior
deltoid
pectoralis major
external oblique
trunk flexors
rectus abdominis
biceps brachii
brachialis
brachoradialis
elbow flexors
tensor fascia lata (hip abductors)
hip adductors
hip flexors
quadriceps (knee extensors)
tibialis anterior

sternocleidomastoid
trapezius
deltoid
infraspinatus
teres minor
teres major
latissimus dorsi
triceps brachi (elbow extensors)
trunk extensors
internal oblique
tensor fascia lata
gluteus medius (hip abductors)
gluteus maximus (hip extensors)
hamstrings (knee flexors)
plantaris
gastrocnemius
soleus
peroneals

The muscular system moves the skeleton. It is made up of muscles. Muscles perform several tasks. These include moving the skeleton, helping to control respiration, and moving the tongue and lips when we talk.

Joints that Move

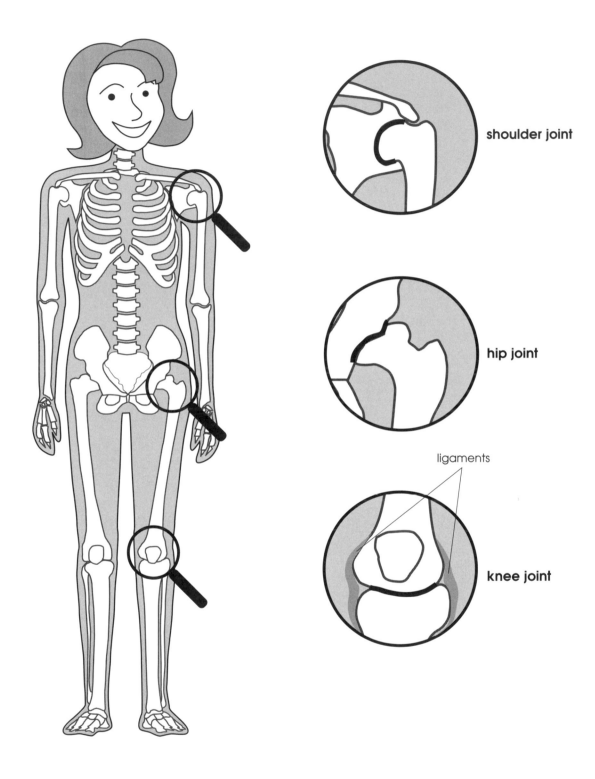

shoulder joint

hip joint

ligaments

knee joint

Bones articulate with other bones at joints. Some joints move and others don't. The shoulder, hip, and knee joints are examples of joints that move. Some joints move more than others, but it is important that joints are stable. Articulating bones are connected by strong, dense attachments called ligaments. Ligaments help to stabilize joints. Strengthening muscles that surround joints through regular and appropriate exercise helps to keep joints stronger, more stable, and injury-free.

Cartilage

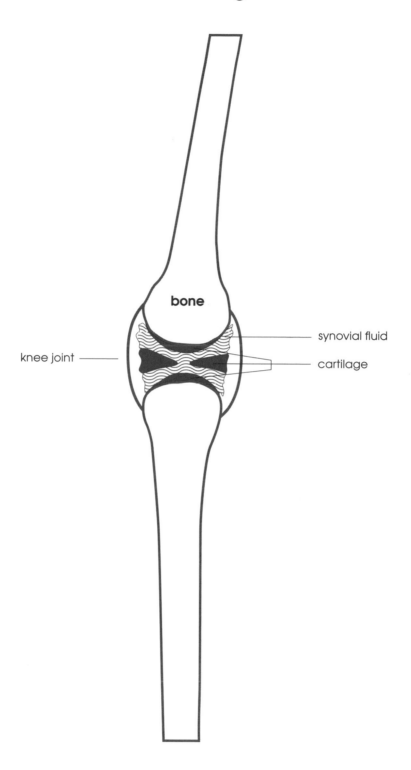

bone

synovial fluid

knee joint

cartilage

A specialized material called cartilage is found where bones articulate at joints. There are different types of cartilage. Some types of cartilage help to protect bones against damage caused by the friction of bones rubbing against each other. Other types act as shock absorbers at joints that receive extra stress from activities that involve impact. As added protection, a liquid material called synovial fluid surrounds some joints. Synovial fluid also helps make movement smoother.

Tendons

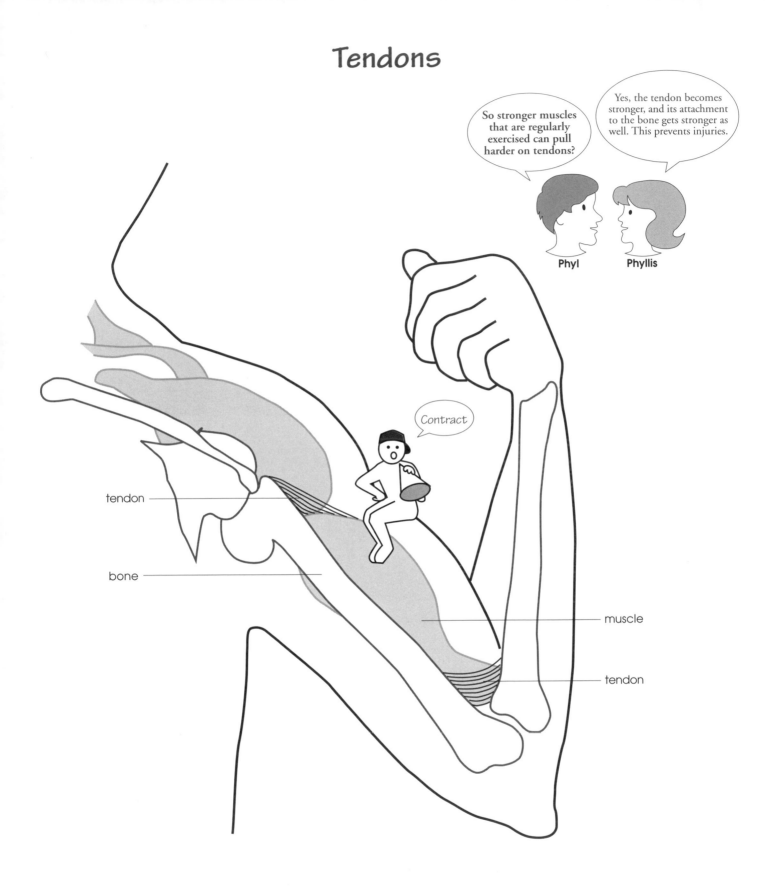

Muscles are attached to bones by rope-like materials called tendons. When the brain or spinal cord sends a message to a muscle to move, the muscle shortens or contracts. This pulls on the tendon, which moves the bone to which it is attached.

Muscle, Bones, and Related Tissues

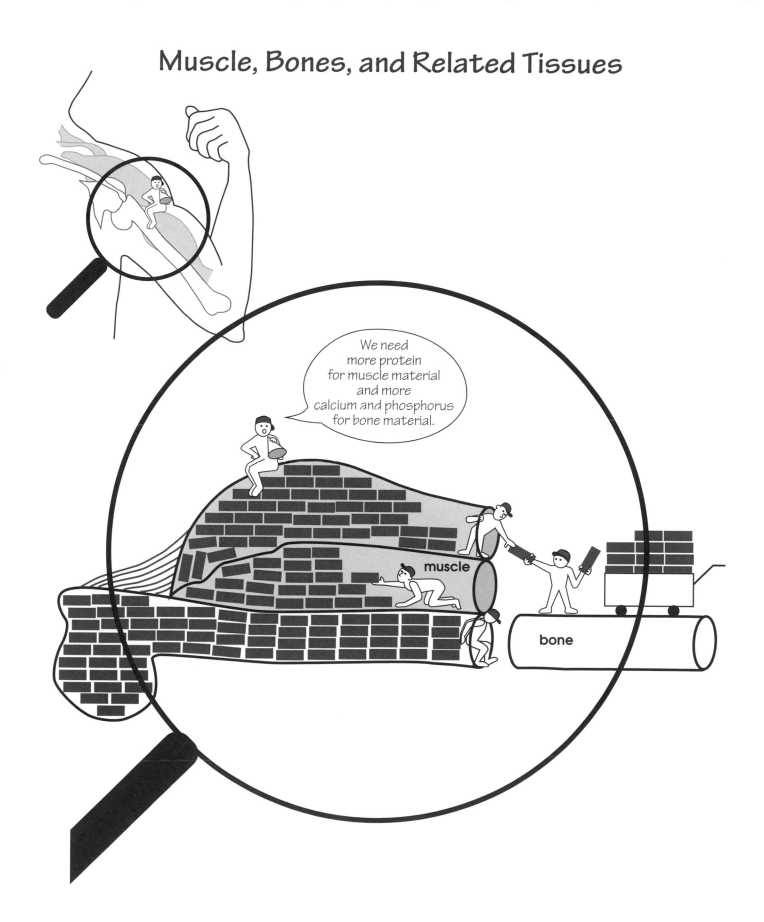

Muscles, bones, and related tissues that are used for work on a regular basis will grow larger and denser. The human body makes what it needs to do work, given adequate nutrition, exercise, and rest.

The Body's Systems

Chapter 3
The Cardiovascular System

The Cardiovascular System

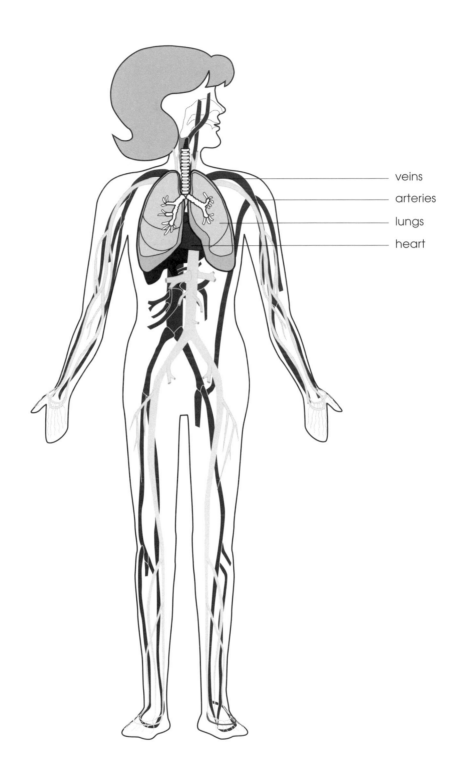

veins

arteries

lungs

heart

The cardiovascular system consists of the heart muscle and the blood vessels, the arteries and veins. The heart is a strong, four-chambered muscular pump that has two jobs. The heart pumps blood to the lungs for gas exchange and it pumps oxygen-rich blood through the body. The lungs move air into and out of the body.

Blood Flow to Active Cell

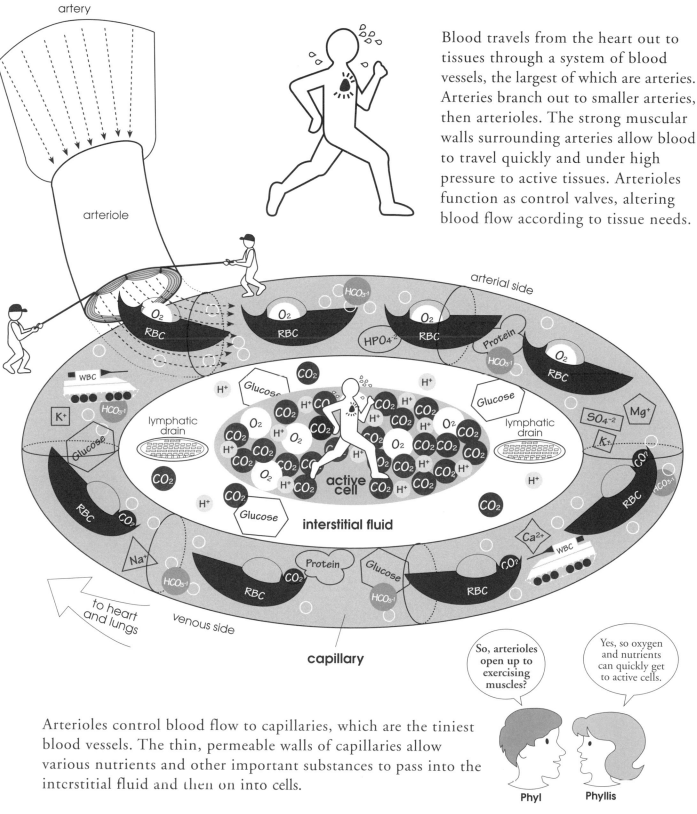

Blood travels from the heart out to tissues through a system of blood vessels, the largest of which are arteries. Arteries branch out to smaller arteries, then arterioles. The strong muscular walls surrounding arteries allow blood to travel quickly and under high pressure to active tissues. Arterioles function as control valves, altering blood flow according to tissue needs.

Arterioles control blood flow to capillaries, which are the tiniest blood vessels. The thin, permeable walls of capillaries allow various nutrients and other important substances to pass into the interstitial fluid and then on into cells.

Interstitial fluid is the fluid that occurs between the blood vessels and tissues. If excessive fluid and materials pass into interstitial spaces from capillaries, there is an alternate drainage system that accepts this overflow. This is called the lymphatic system. The lymphatic system operates throughout the body and empties materials into the body's larger veins.

27

Blood Flow to Inactive Cell

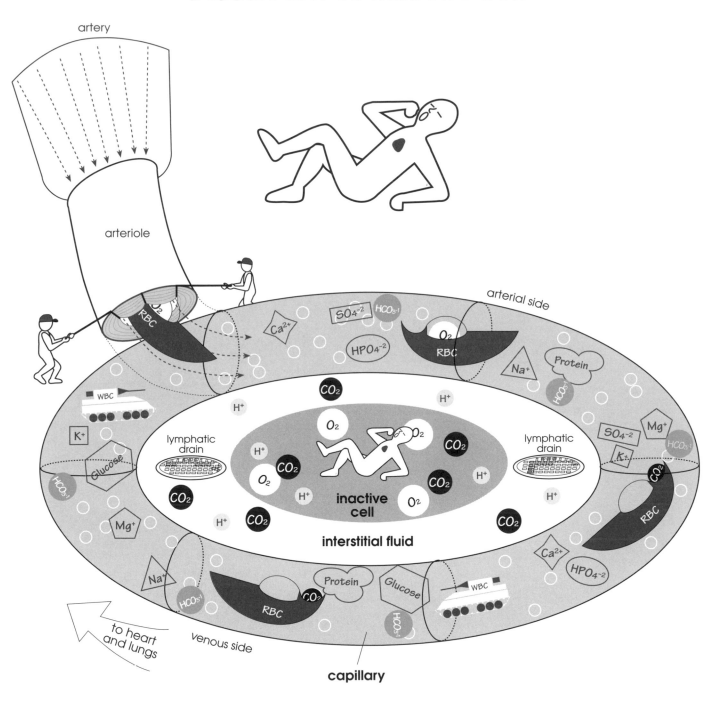

After capillaries deliver materials to tissue cells, blood is collected in tiny venules, which gradually progress into large veins. The venous system returns blood to the heart and lungs.

Active tissues receive lots of blood and less active tissues receive less blood. The body makes sure that there is enough blood to serve its tissues as tissues need it. Active tissues return blood through the venous system to the heart and lungs quickly. The heart muscle pumps as much blood as it receives as fast as the blood returns.

The Heart and Lungs

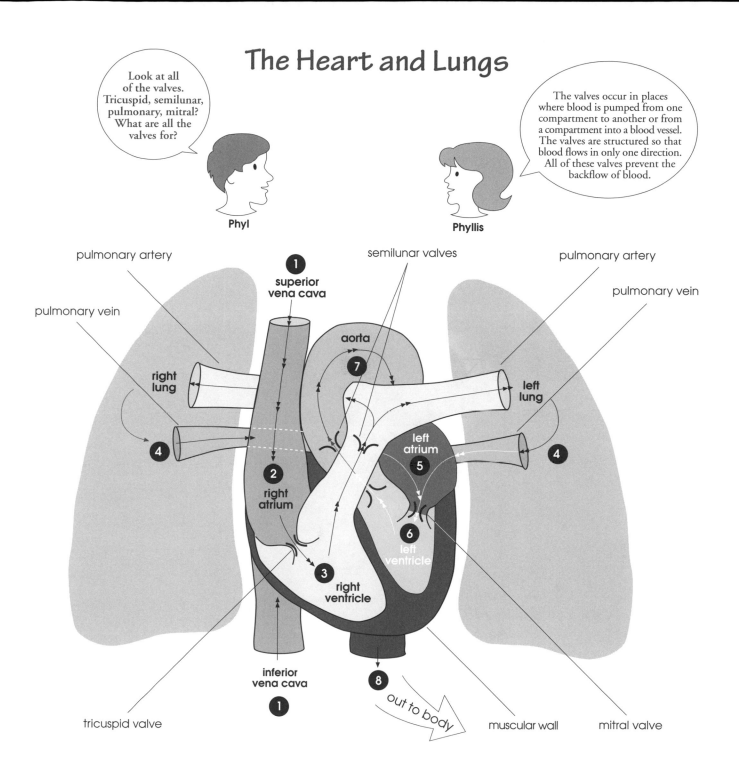

The heart receives blood from body parts as quickly or as slowly as the body is moving. Blood from the body's working muscles enters the heart from the inferior and superior vena cavae, which are the body's largest veins.

Blood enters the first chamber, the right atrium. Then it is pumped into the right ventricle. The blood is then pumped to the lungs through the pulmonary arteries to receive oxygen. The oxygenated blood reenters the heart through the pulmonary veins into the left atrium and is then pumped into the left ventricle.

The strong muscular walls of the left ventricle pump the blood into the body's largest artery, the aorta, and from there out to all of the body's tissues and organs.

29

The Lungs

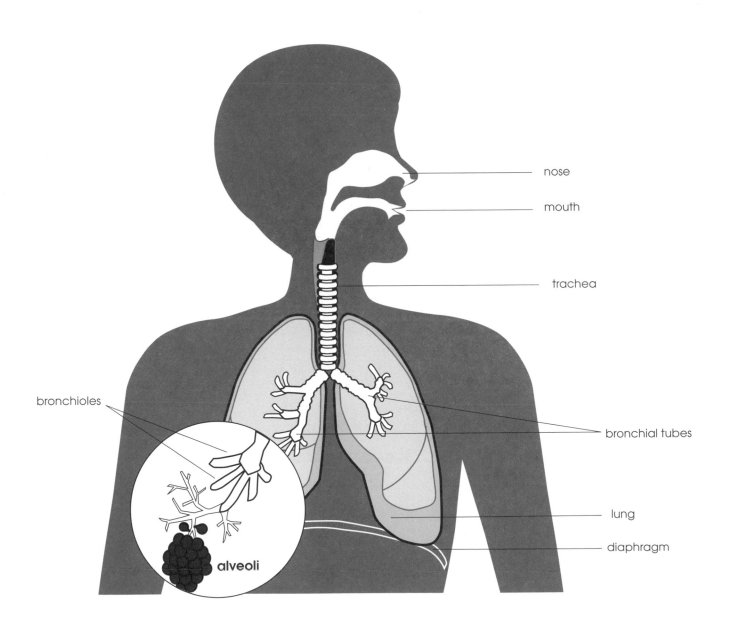

The lungs move air from the atmosphere into and out of the body as a result of the movement of a large, dome-shaped muscle called the diaphragm and other breathing muscles. Air enters our bodies through our noses and mouths when we inhale. The air moves into the trachea through bronchial tubes. The air then travels deep into the lungs to tiny grape-like structures called alveoli.

The Lung Alveolus

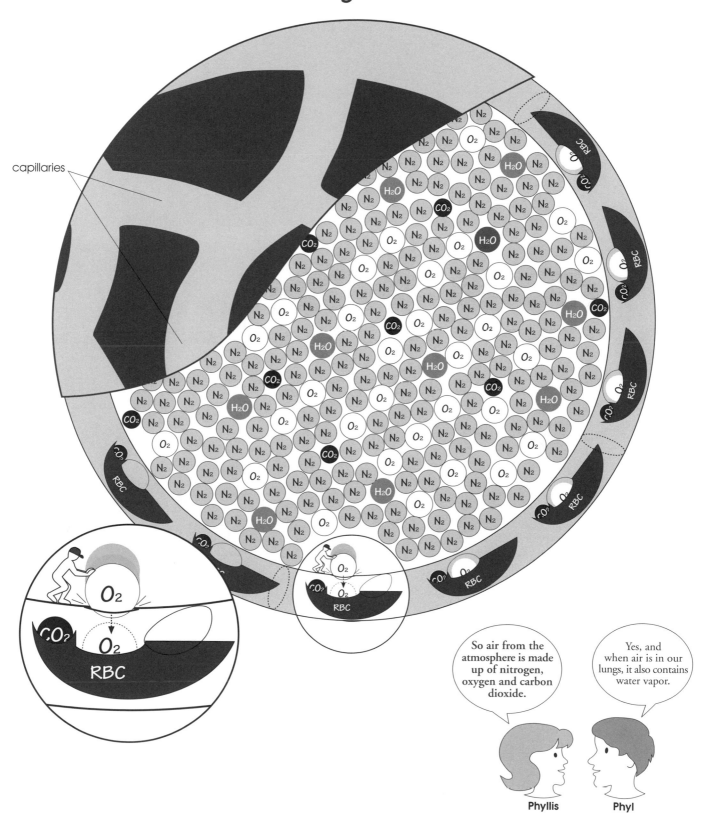

The alveoli of the lungs are covered with capillaries. The oxygen from the air enters the capillaries at the alveoli and is carried in red blood cells (RBCs) to the heart. The oxygenated blood is then pumped through the aorta, out to all of the tissues of the body including to the heart muscle itself.

Oxygen Delivery into the Cell; Carbon Dioxide Removal from the Cell

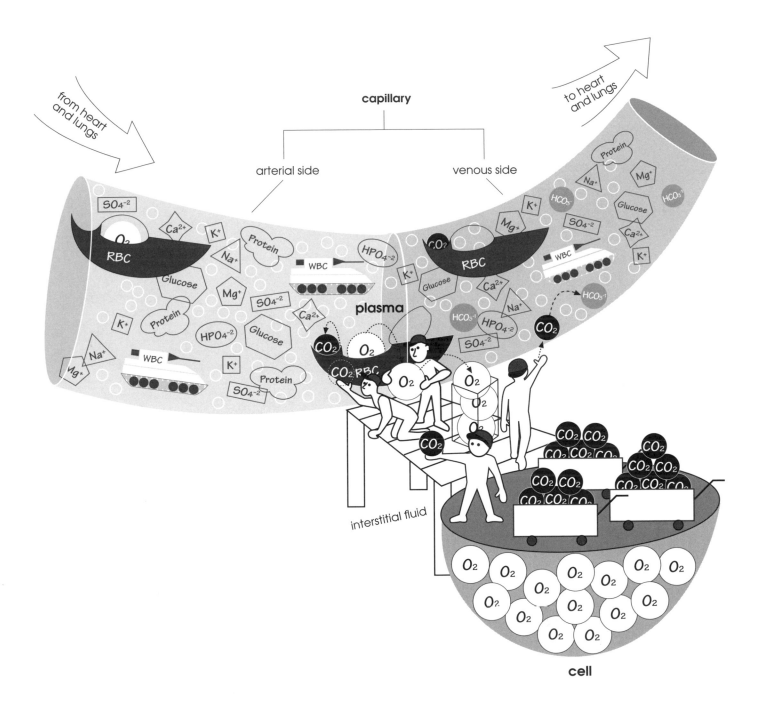

When RBCs bring oxygen to our tissue cells, the tissue cells return carbon dioxide to the blood. Deoxygenated blood that enters the lungs carries carbon dioxide back out into the atmosphere when we exhale.

Healthy and Damaged Heart and Lungs

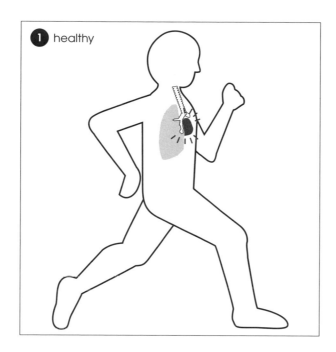

Healthy, exercised lungs have healthy blood vessels. They bring more oxygen into the blood. Damaged lungs or those that are not exercised do not do this very well. Smoking causes severe damage to healthy lungs.

A moving, exercising body sends more blood to the heart muscle more quickly. A heart that receives more blood pumps blood faster and harder. Regular exercise creates a strong heart muscle that does this job very well.

The Body's Systems

Chapter 4
How Systems Work Together

Initiation of Movement

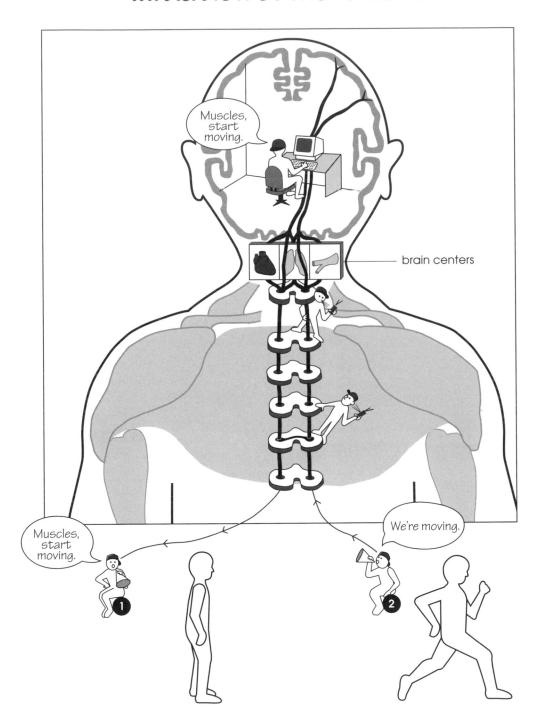

brain centers

How do all the systems of the body work together when we exercise?

An area in the brain has centers in it that control such involuntary tissues and organs as the heart, the lungs, and the blood vessels. These centers are called the cardioacceleratory center, the respiratory center, and the vasomotor center. These centers send messages along the autonomic efferent wiring system.

Exercise is initiated when our brain tells our muscles via efferent somatic nerves to move. The appropriate muscles begin to move and they send a message to the brain centers that we are moving.

The Brain Centers

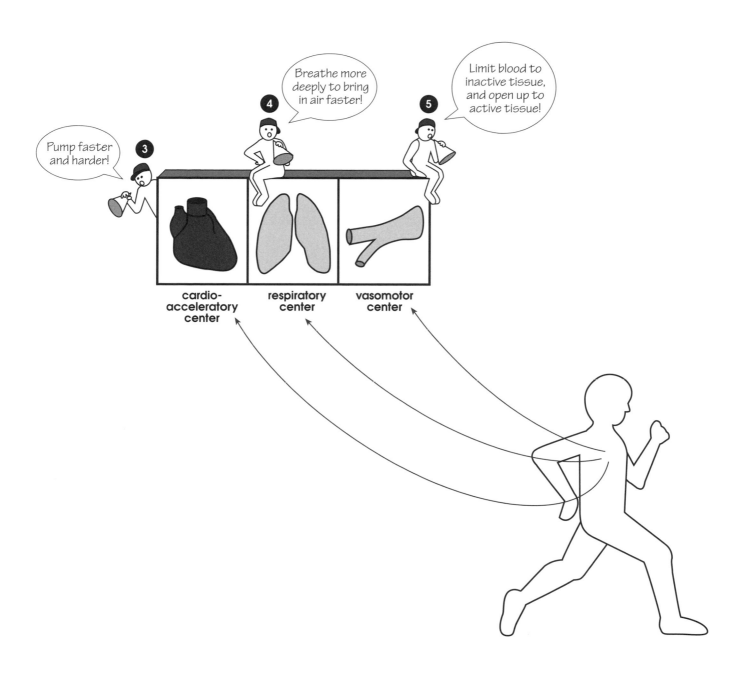

When the cardioacceleratory center is alerted that the body is moving, it sends a message to the heart muscle and tells it to beat faster and pump with greater force.

When the respiratory center receives messages from moving muscles, the breathing muscles are told to bring more air into the lungs at a faster rate.

When the vasomotor center is alerted to the muscular movement, blood vessels in active tissues are told to widen or dilate and blood vessels in less active tissues are told to narrow or constrict.

The Adrenal Medulla:
Production of Epinephrine and Norepinephrine

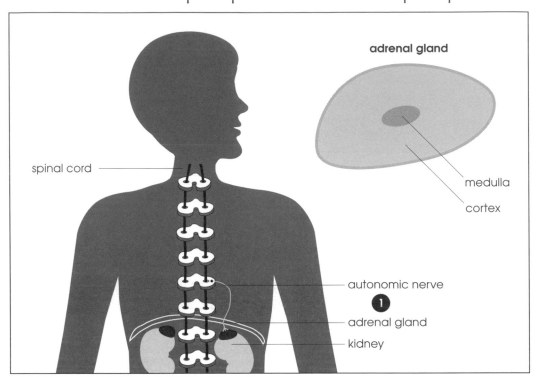

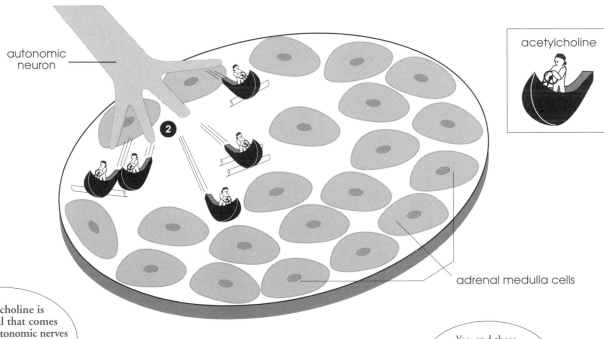

So acetylcholine is the chemical that comes out of these autonomic nerves and causes epinephrine and norepinephrine to squirt out into the blood.

Yes, and these hormones travel in the blood to target organs such as the heart, blood vessels, and bronchioles, etc.

Phyllis

Phyl

While all of this is going on, other autonomic nerves stimulate the adrenal gland, located on the kidney. In response, the central part of the adrenal gland, the medulla, secretes epinephrine or adrenalin and norepinephrine or noradrenalin.

Epinephrine and Norepinephrine
in the Blood

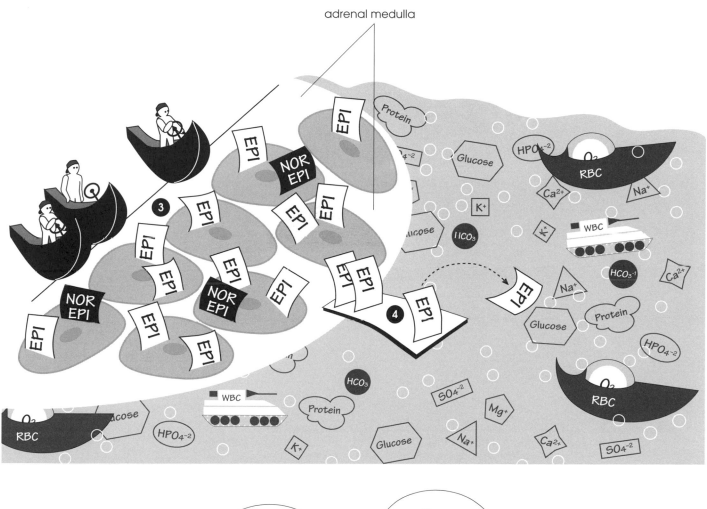

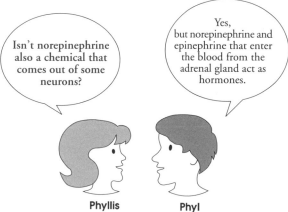

Epinephrine and norepinephrine are hormones that are secreted into the blood. They travel in the blood to all of the tissues and organs of the body. These hormones cause the heart muscle to pump faster and harder. They cause increased dilation of bronchioles, which allows for greater air flow to the lungs. They cause dilation of blood vessels leading to working muscles and constriction of blood vessels leading to inactive tissues.

Actions of Epinephrine and Norepinephrine
in the Body

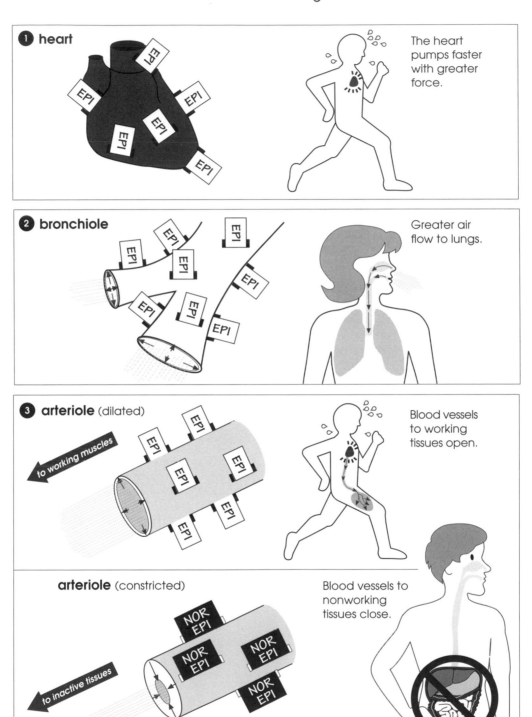

1 heart — The heart pumps faster with greater force.

2 bronchiole — Greater air flow to lungs.

3 arteriole (dilated) — Blood vessels to working tissues open.
to working muscles

arteriole (constricted) — Blood vessels to nonworking tissues close.
to inactive tissues

All of these responses collectively increase the oxygen supply to exercising muscles. The adrenal hormones work along with the autonomic nervous system to support optimal body function during exercise.

Epinephrine also causes the mobilization of fuel stores in our liver and fat cells. How does the human body use fuel? What does it use for fuel?

The Mitochondrion
The Production of ATP from Energy-Yielding Nutrients

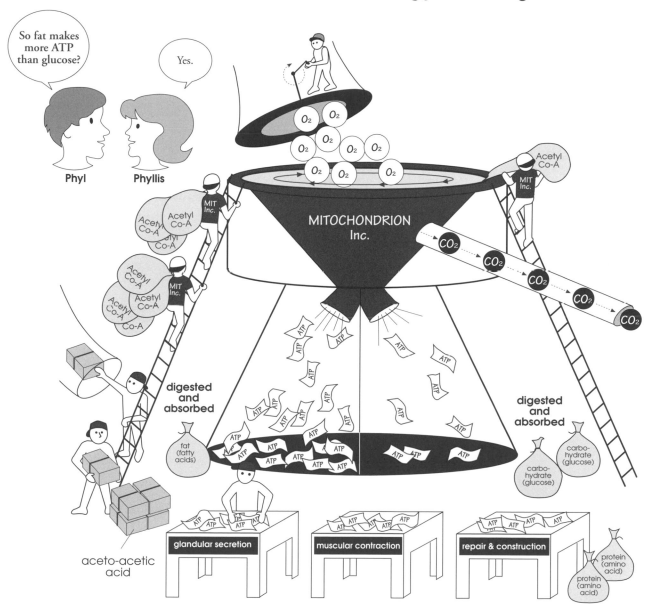

The muscle and tissue cells in our bodies perform work using the energy obtained from a chemical compound called adenosine-triphosphate, or ATP. This high-energy compound is the primary energy "currency" of the human body. It is made inside cells in organelles called mitochondria. ATP is made from the breakdown of nutrients contained in the foods we eat.

Those nutrients that make up the bulk of the diet are called macronutrients; those that occur in foods in very small quantities are called micronutrients. Carbohydrates, fats, protein, water, and some minerals are macronutrients. Vitamins and minerals, referred to as "trace" minerals, are micronutrients.

The macronutrients that yield energy or ATP are carbohydrates, fats, and protein. While the presence of vitamins, minerals, and water are important in several biological processes throughout the body, these nutrients do not yield energy.

Common Structural Elements
of Energy-Yielding Nutrients

Glucose Structure

$$H-C=O$$
$$OH-C-H$$
$$H-C-OH$$
$$H-C-OH$$
$$H-C-OH$$
$$H$$

=

Glucose

Protein Structure

$$H-N-C-C-OH$$
with H, H, O

varies from protein to protein

=

Amino Acid

Fatty Acid Structure

glycerol

$$H-C-O-C$$
$$H-C-O-C$$
$$H-C-O-C$$

fatty acid chains

=

Glycerol

All of the foods we eat are made up of a variety of nutrients. Each nutrient is made up of different chemical compounds, each of which is combined in various quantities and proportions. Each of the chemical compounds is comprised of basic building blocks or chemical components. The energy-yielding macronutrients, carbohydrates and fats are made up of carbon, hydrogen, and oxygen atoms. Protein is comprised of all three of these along with nitrogen atoms.

During times when food is unavailable, the liver can arrange and rearrange chemical structures and substances that are present within the body to synthesize several important nutrients. However, there are nutrients that cannot be made in sufficient quantities to maintain, repair, or build body tissues and sustain cellular functions. Therefore they must be eaten in foods. Such nutrients are called essential nutrients.

The body is dependent on specific quantities of each of the essential nutrients to meet its physiological needs. Essential amino acids combine with other amino acids in specific proportions to build proteins that make up many of the body's tissues, carriers, neurotransmitters, hormones, and other important materials. Essential fatty acids are important for several important structures and functions.

The Digestive System

Digestion breaks food into its smallest components so that it may be absorbed. Carbohydrate digestion begins in the mouth. Protein digestion begins in the stomach. Most digestion and absorption of nutrients takes place at the small intestine.

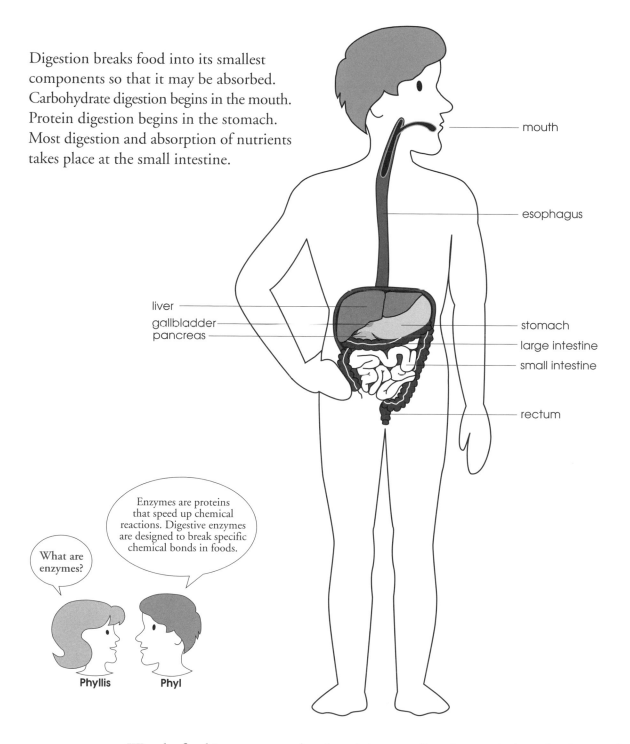

mouth

esophagus

liver
gallbladder
pancreas

stomach
large intestine
small intestine

rectum

What are enzymes?

Enzymes are proteins that speed up chemical reactions. Digestive enzymes are designed to break specific chemical bonds in foods.

Phyllis   **Phyl**

We take food into our mouths, chew it into smaller pieces, mix it with saliva, and swallow it. It travels down the esophagus into the stomach. In the stomach, it is mixed up, churned, and doused with various substances that prepare it for digestion.

Food is digested by enzymes that are designed to break up specific types of chemical bonds that occur in carbohydrates, proteins, and fats. Most of these enzymes are secreted into the small intestine by the pancreas. Secreting digestive enzymes is just one of the jobs of the pancreas.

The Kidney

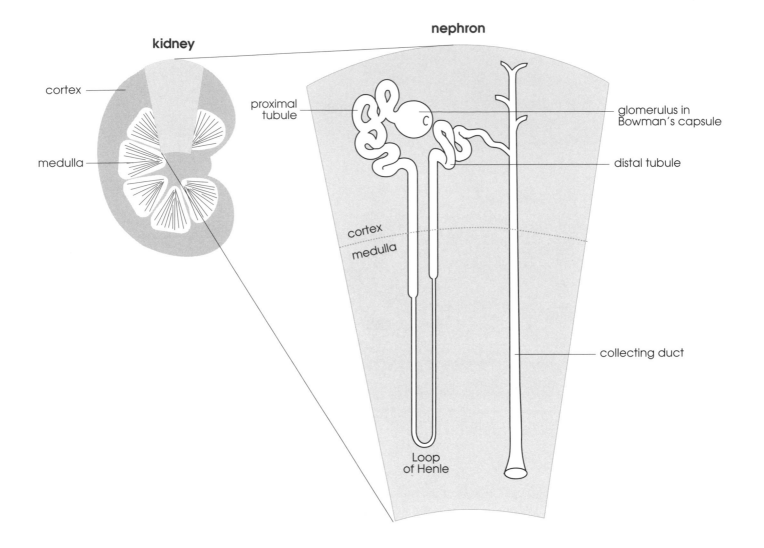

kidney

cortex

medulla

nephron

proximal tubule

glomerulus in Bowman's capsule

distal tubule

cortex

medulla

collecting duct

Loop of Henle

Carbohydrates, fats, and proteins are digested and absorbed into the blood at the small intestine. The digested and absorbed nutrients are transported in the blood to and from cells along with many other substances. As cells perform their work, the resulting waste products are also transported in the blood and carried to the two kidneys.

In the kidneys, the blood is filtered through a complex system of nephrons. Nephrons are the functional units of the kidneys. They consist of a glomerulus, a sac-like structure containing a network of capillaries through which the blood is filtered, and a tubular structure that transforms the filtered materials into urine. Red blood cells and blood plasma proteins do not pass into the tubules as they are too large.

Each nephron is designed to reabsorb water and other substances that the body needs to retain and to excrete waste products in the urine. In this way, the constitution of blood is closely monitored and kept consistent.

What is heart rate?
What is resting heart rate?
How do I know my maximum heart rate?

Phyl and Phyllis's Physiology Phorum

Heart rate is the number of times the heart beats per minute. Resting heart rate is the number of times the heart beats when a person is not physically active. Normal resting heart rates range from sixty to eighty beats per minute. The heart muscle has its own electrical system that rhythmically and continuously creates its own beat. This system and the heart muscle itself are influenced by autonomic nerves. They are also influenced by the action of adrenalin or epinephrine. The heart rate can be slowed or increased depending on the needs of the tissues as they perform particular activities.

Theoretically, maximum heart rate is related to an individual's age. At birth, the heart can beat as fast as 220 beats per minute. Each year thereafter, the maximum heart rate declines by one beat. At age twenty, for example, the maximum heart rate should be 200 beats per minute. Each person, however, has his or her own maximum heart rate. It can vary by as much as ten to fifteen beats per minute from one person to another of the same age.

Heart Rate

 **1** pulse at carotid artery

2 pulse at radial artery

3 pulse with heart monitors

Heart rate can be measured by taking one's pulse at either the carotid artery located on the side of the neck, or at the radial artery located at the wrist on the thumb side. There are also electronic heart monitors that can be used to measure heart rate during activity.

What is cardiovascular exercise?

What should my heart rate be during this type of exercise?

What is perceived rate of exertion (RPE)?

Phyl and Phyllis's Physiology Phorum

During cardiovascular exercise, the heart must pump blood to large muscles in the body, when a person is moving in a rhythmical pattern continuously for a period of time. The duration depends on an individual's ability to sustain an activity. Walking, jogging, running, swimming, Rollerblading, cycling, and dancing are examples of cardiovascular exercise.

How much cardiovascular exercise one needs depends upon individual goals. However, the American College of Sports Medicine (ACSM) and the American Council on Exercise (ACE) recommend 20 to 60 minutes of cardiovascular activity from three to five days per week. It is important to note that a cardiovascular activity need not be performed all at one time, but in fact, can be accumulated over multiple sessions. The duration and intensity of exercise depend on the fitness level of the individual performing them. Individuals striving for weight loss should exercise for 60 minutes or longer at a low to moderate intensity at least five days a week. Higher fitness goals require the performance of activities at a higher intensity. Athletes with specific performance goals must work at intensities that mimic their sport. Most importantly, cardiovascular activities should be enjoyable, varied, and suited to an individual's lifestyle and goals.

Heart rate during cardiovascular exercise is related to the specific energy requirements of different activities. It takes a specific amount of energy (in the form of ATP) for a particular body to perform a given activity. For example, less ATP is required to walk four miles per hour than to run seven miles per hour. Red blood cells must load up appropriate quantities of oxygen to send to tissues performing that activity. The heart must then pump oxygen-laden red blood cells to these tissue cells rapidly enough to deliver the required oxygen.

In the tissue cell mitochondria, oxygen is required to make ATP. ATP is used to fuel the activity. Heart rates vary from person to person and depend on the intensity and energy requirements of a given activity.

There are many different formulas that are used to determine heart rate ranges for different activities. While heart rate is a reliable and accurate estimate of intensity, there are some limitations to using it. There are factors that can affect heart rate other than the energy requirements of an activity itself.

Heart rates can be increased by hot and humid temperatures. They can also be affected by an individual's skill levels, body mechanics, and experience performing particular activities. Some medications may alter heart rate in such a way that its measurement might not be a reliable indicator of the intensity of an exercise. Lack of sleep, stress level, and even how a person feels on a given day can change his or her heart rate.

For these reasons, other methods were developed and are frequently used to monitor the intensity of cardiovascular activity. One such method is called the Borg scale of perceived rate of exertion (RPE). Borg's scale uses numbers ranging from six to twenty, in which six represents no exertion and twenty represents maximal effort.

The numbers permit individuals to describe how difficult an activity feels to them. For example, an activity that causes a great deal of sweating, labored breathing, and muscle fatigue might be perceived as "very hard." That would be given a rating of 18 on the Borg scale. Movement that feels effortless may be perceived as "fairly light" and given a rating of 11. Both scenarios would require an adjustment to a more appropriate intensity.

Paying close attention to how one feels while performing a given activity allows for such an adjustment. For example, by speeding up, adding a grade, or increasing the size of movement, an activity can intensify from fairly light (11) to somewhat hard (13). In order to achieve the important benefits of cardiovascular activity, ACSM and ACE recommend 60 to 85 percent of maximum heart rate or ratings of 13 to 15 on the Borg scale.

However, novices should begin a cardiovascular program wisely, beginning at lower levels and gradually progressing to higher levels over time. Progress will depend on the individual's age, fitness level, starting goals, and other factors such as time constraints and lifestyle. Appropriate health screening is highly recommended before starting any exercise program.

A beginner may work at slightly less than 60 percent of his or her maximum heart rate (11 on the scale). An avid exerciser may regularly perform at 80 to 90 percent of his or her maximum heart rate (15 to 16 on the scale). A non-athlete should try to exercise consistently, performing different and challenging activities at varying levels each week. Heart rate ranges and RPEs should simply be used as guidelines.

Perceived Rate of Exertion (Borg Scale)		Percent of VO2 Max
6		
7	very, very light	
8		
9	very light	
10		42%
11	fairly light	
12		56%
13	somewhat hard	
14		70%
15	hard	
16		83%
17	very hard	
18		88%
19	very, very hard	
20		100%

What are the components of a good cardiovascular exercise program?

What is aerobic capacity?

How do I know if I've improved my aerobic capacity?

Phyl and Phyllis's Physiology Phorum

A good cardiovascular exercise program consists of three phases: a warm-up phase, a cardiovascular work phase, and a cool-down phase. The warm-up phase introduces the upcoming movements. It consists of large, rhythmical movements similar to the upcoming activity. The movements are performed at a low level for about five minutes.

This phase may or may not include stretching. It depends on the cardiovascular activity that will follow it. For example, if the activity is one that involves a great deal of quick or sudden stretching of muscles, such as running or dancing, it may be a good idea to introduce a type of stretching called dynamic stretching, in the warm-up phase. If it will help in the smoother, safer performance of the cardiovascular activity that will follow, a time-efficient dynamic stretching routine preceding that activity is worthwhile. Otherwise, stretching can be performed following the cardiovascular work in the cool-down phase.

Warm-Up

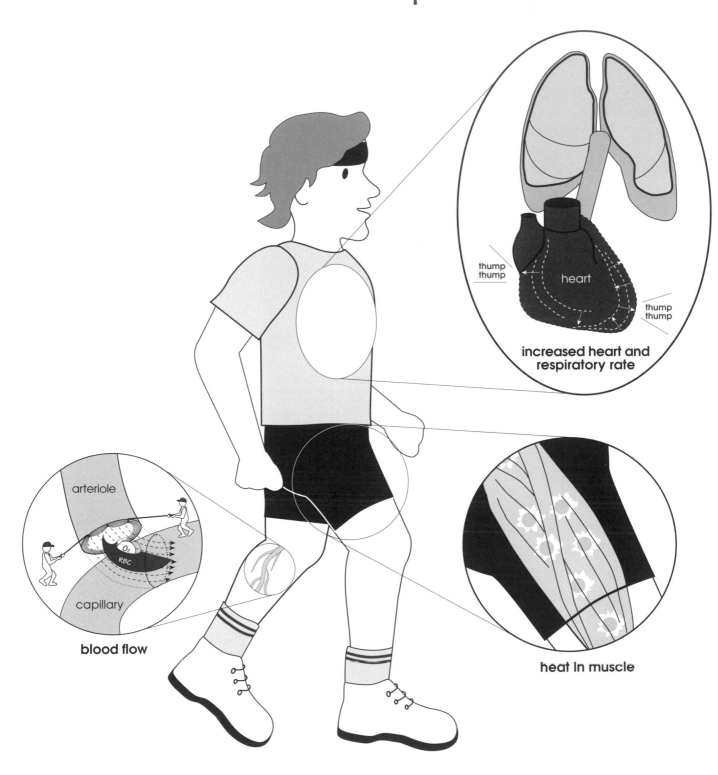

increased heart and respiratory rate

heart

thump thump

thump thump

arteriole

capillary

RBC

O₂

blood flow

heat in muscle

The warm-up phase allows the heart rate and respiratory rate to increase gradually. It helps the skeletal and muscular systems process and coordinate the information sent to and from the central nervous system. It allows the muscles to begin work gradually, receiving blood, nutrients, and oxygen from the blood vessels. As the muscles begin to work, heat is produced, warming both the muscle tissue itself and the fluid surrounding joints. This allows for smoother movement.

Work Phase

The cardiovascular work phase consists of an activity that is sustained at a particular intensity or variety of intensities for a desired duration. Both the duration and the intensity depend on individual goals. Walking, jogging, running, biking, hiking, swimming, and dancing are all cardiovascular activities. Beginners may only be able to sustain a brisk walk for twenty minutes. An athletic individual may run for an hour or more.

Performing different cardiovascular activities during the course of a week provides an individual with variety. It also allows for cardiovascular training that uses different movement patterns. This rotation of different activities is called cross-training. Cross-training helps to prevent overuse injuries in muscle and connective tissues. It allows all of the activities to seem "fresh" to the nervous and muscular systems as well.

During the cardiovascular work phase, the heart pumps blood through the arterial system to working muscles. Blood returns by way of the venous system. When muscles rhythmically contract, they compress the veins in the same rhythmical pattern. This rhythmical contraction of the moving muscles helps to pump blood in the veins back up to the heart. This rhythmical contraction also pushes waste products from working muscles out of the muscle into the venous system.

Veins are equipped with a system of one-way valves. The valves both promote the blood flow back to the heart and prevent a back-flow. After the cardiovascular work period, the rapidly beating heart must return gradually to its resting rate. A cool-down period is therefore essential.

Cool-Down

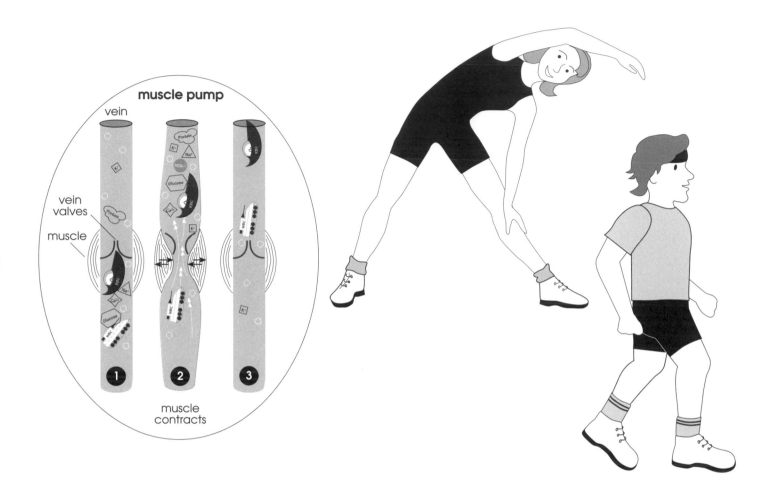

The return of blood by way of the veins to the heart occurs as rapidly or as slowly as the working muscles contract. The heart rate adjusts to the speed of venous return of blood. Gradual slowing of movement allows for gradual slowing of blood return as well as gradual slowing of heart rate. The waste produced by the working muscles continues to leave the muscles as long as they contract. Blood and waste products pool in the working muscles if movement is suddenly halted.

A five-minute cool-down period prevents pooling of blood and waste products in muscles. A static stretching program may follow the cool-down period. Static stretches are those that are held for fifteen to thirty seconds. Appropriate static stretches may help return muscles and other connective tissues to their normal resting length. This may help to improve the flexibility in areas of chronic tightness, such as the lower back, front of the hips, the back of the thighs and back of the calves. It may also help to improve range of motion in performing tasks of daily living and sports, posture and maintenance of proper body alignment. Some activities emphasize the use of some muscle groups not used in other activities. Running, biking, swimming, walking, and dancing each require distinct movement patterns. Different activities may be followed by different stretching routines.

Sample Stretches

BASIC STATIC STRETCHES: Gently hold for 15 to 30 seconds

BACK
(Lower back)

Bring each knee into chest separately, then both knees together

Drop bent knees to right side, then left

Cat n' Camel (lower back and trunk mobility)

HAMSTRINGS
(Back of thigh)

Lean into straightened leg with straight back

with band

QUADRICEPS
(Front of thigh and front of hip)

Bend knee and pull leg up behind you toward your back side

A more important benefit of regular participation in cardiovascular exercise is reduction of the risk of cardiovascular and other diseases. Another is increased aerobic capacity. Aerobic capacity is the maximum amount of oxygen utilized by the body per minute per body weight. Regular cardiovascular exercise improves capillary function at the lung alveolus so that more oxygen is picked up by red blood cells. Exercise improves the function of the heart, creating a stronger pump that allows for greater quantities of blood to be pumped with each beat. The heart can then beat fewer times and can spend more time resting and filling with blood.

With increased aerobic capacity, more blood vessels branch out closer to the cells that they serve. Inside the cell, more mitochondria are made to handle the increased ATP demands of consistently active tissue. More oxygen is therefore brought into cells at a faster rate. This means the cell is better equipped to utilize fat to make ATP. The body becomes a better fat burner.

Sample Stretches

BASIC STATIC STRETCHES: Gently hold for 15 to 30 seconds

CALVES
1. Gastrocnemius
   (surface muscles)
2. Soleus (underneath muscles)

1. straight back leg   2. bent back leg

CHEST AND FRONT OF SHOULDER

Turn away from wall, arm is at shoulder level

UPPER BACK AND BACK OF SHOULDER

Hold onto a band or pole and pull back, bring chin to chest

Tilt head forward, cross arm and pull shoulders apart (like you are hugging yourself)

TRICEPS AND BACK (Lats*)
* Latissimus dorsi

Raise arm straight, bend elbow to touch shoulder, push elbow with opposite hand

Improvement in aerobic capacity, practically speaking, is reflected in the greater ease with which activities are performed. Tasks of daily living require less effort. For example, we no longer become winded or fatigued walking up and down stairs, to and from a train station, or to a bus stop. We can rush through an airport to a distant gate to catch a plane. We can dance longer at weddings or other celebrations. Participation in regular cardiovascular exercise prevents disease, improves aerobic capacity, creates a leaner and healthier body, and generally improves quality of life. It is essential therefore that one follow the ACSM and ACE guidelines and integrate a cardiovascular exercise program into daily life. The following are some tips for planning a cardiovascular exercise program. The five-day "lifestyle-integrated" program below illustrates how one might plan a week of cardiovascular activities for the family.

Tips for Planning a Cardiovascular Exercise Program

- Set achievable, realistic, long-term and short-term goals while following ACSM and ACE guidelines.

- Be consistent; schedule cardiovascular activity into your day like any other appointment and keep it.

- Add elements of change and challenge. For your cardiovascular routine to remain effective, progress over time and cross-train (regularly change the equipment and/or activity to prevent overuse injuries).

- Make it enjoyable; if you don't particularly like the cardiovascular activity itself, connect it with activities you do enjoy, i.e., reading, listening to music, watching your favorite television shows or visiting with or phoning friends and family members.

A Five-Day Lifestyle-Integrated Family Cardiovascular Exercise Program*

Sunday ... 60-minute, 6-to10-mile family bike ride to and from a specified destination

Monday ... 30-minute brisk walk on a treadmill (gym or home) to the evening news or favorite CD; one can perform higher level intervals using increased speed or grade during commercials, or every other song on the CD

Tuesday ... Off

Wednesday ... 2.5-mile walk to and from dinner at neighborhood restaurant

Thursday ... 30-minute jog on treadmill (gym or home) to favorite television program

Friday ... Off

Saturday ... 60-minute cross-training; outdoors or indoors

Outdoors – walk, jog, run, bike, rollerblade
Indoors – aerobics, step, cardio-kickboxing, dance or spinning, walk, jog, run, cycle, or elliptical trainer

Before participating in any exercise make sure to be cleared by your family physician.
Carry a bottle of water with you and be sure to tell a responsible person where you are going if you are exercising alone.

Essential Nutrients

Chapter 5
Carbohydrates

Photosynthesis

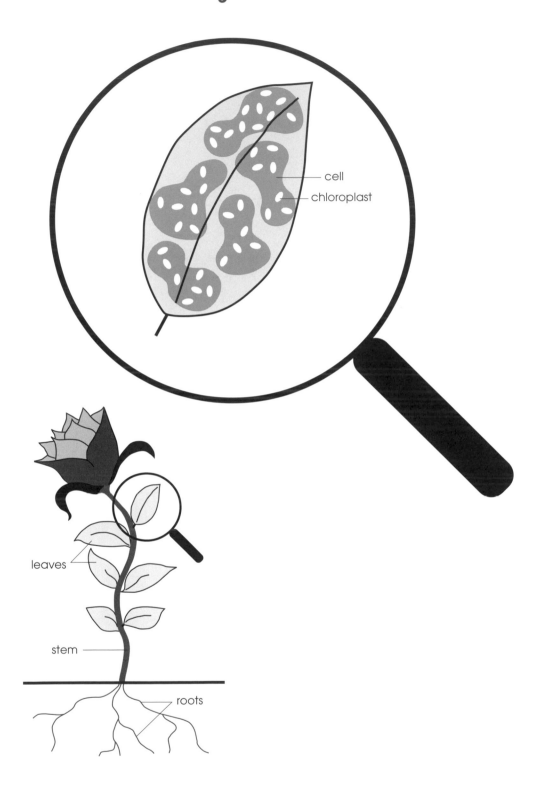

Carbohydrates come from plants such as the fruits, vegetables, and grains that we eat. These plants grow in the sunlight. The energy from the sunlight is captured in their leaves. There are tiny sac-like cells in the leaves of plants. These cells contain food-making entities called chloroplasts. Chloroplasts are filled with chlorophyll.

Photosynthesis:
The Making of Starch

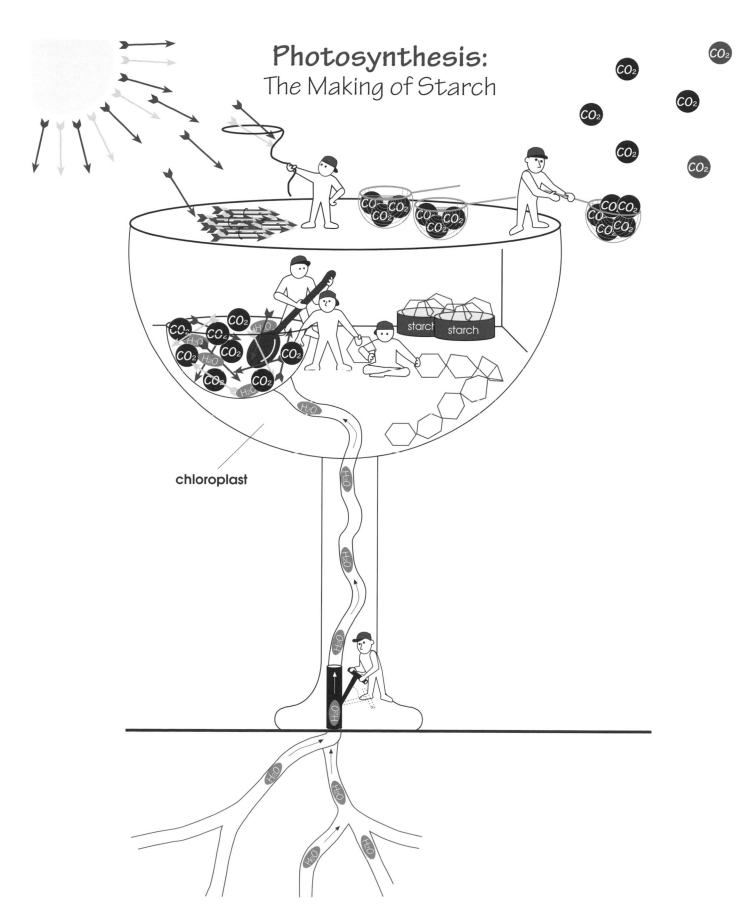

By a process called photosynthesis, chloroplasts use the energy captured by chlorophyll from the sun's light and combine carbon dioxide from the air with water from the plant's roots to make starch. Starch is one form of carbohydrate.

Sugar Molecules

monosaccharide

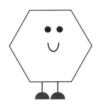

disaccharide

polysaccharide

Carbohydrates consist of sugars, starches and fiber. Sugars may occur as one unit or molecule, called a monosaccharide; or as two molecules, called a disaccharide. All sugar molecules are comprised of carbon, hydrogen, and oxygen atoms. These combine to form unique chemical structures. Starches and fiber occur as polysaccharides, which are several to several hundred or more molecules of sugar branched or linked together.

Those sugars that occur naturally in such foods as whole grains, fruits, vegetables and milks are called intrinsic sugars. Those sugars that are added to foods are called extrinsic sugars, examples of which are white or brown sugar and maple syrup.

Glucose

There are several nutritionally important sugars. Starch and fiber, however, are made up of only one kind of sugar called glucose. Glucose is comprised of carbon, hydrogen, and oxygen atoms that are chemically arranged to form a six-sided structure or hexagon. Glucose is one of the body's most important nutrient sources for making ATP. In addition to the glucose stored and used in muscle cells to fuel activity, glucose supplies the brain and nervous system with a constant energy supply. Since the brain and the nervous system directly or indirectly control almost every body function, their fuel supply must be readily available.

Whole grains, fruits, vegetables, and milks are comprised of sugars, starches, and fiber, as well as a variety of other nutrients. While the sugars and most starches in these foods are broken down into glucose and absorbed at the small intestine, fiber is not. Fiber is like starch in that it is made up of glucose molecules that are linked together. However, the manner in which the glucose molecules are linked in fiber is different from that of starch.

Human digestive enzymes are able to break the chemical bonds that link glucose molecules in starch, thus making the glucose available to be used for energy. There are no human digestive enzymes that are designed to break the chemical bonds in fiber. Therefore, its glucose is not available to make ATP. Thus, most fiber is not digestible and travels relatively intact through the small intestine into the large intestine.

Though not used as fuel, fiber does provide numerous other health-promoting benefits. Both soluble fiber, which mixes well with body fluids, and insoluble fiber, which does not, are nutritionally important. Different foods contain different types of fiber. Soluble fiber—such as that contained in oat bran, barley, nuts, seeds, beans, citrus fruits, apples and numerous vegetables—has been shown to prevent cardiovascular diseases. Insoluble fiber—such as that contained in whole grains, vegetables, and wheat bran—has been shown to aid in digestive health.

Carbohydrate Digestion

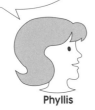

Humans have digestive enzymes that can break up starch into glucose to make ATP.

Phyllis

True. But we do not have the digestive enzymes that can break the bonds in most fiber. The glucose is therefore not available for energy.

Phyl

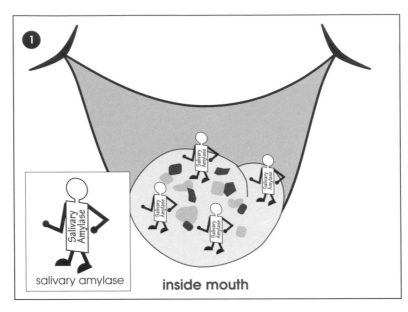

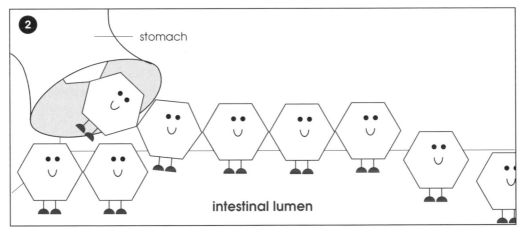

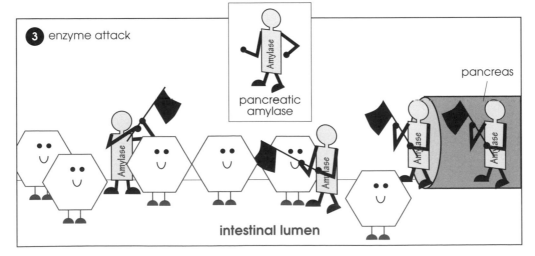

The digestion of many starches begins in the mouth with salivary enzymes (salivary amylase) and typically ends at the small intestine with pancreatic enzymes (pancreatic amylase). There are many different types of starch, and each is digested and absorbed in its own way.

Carbohydrate Absorption

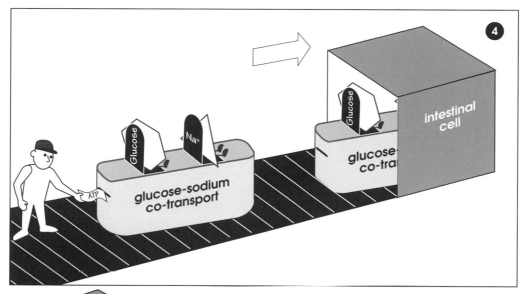

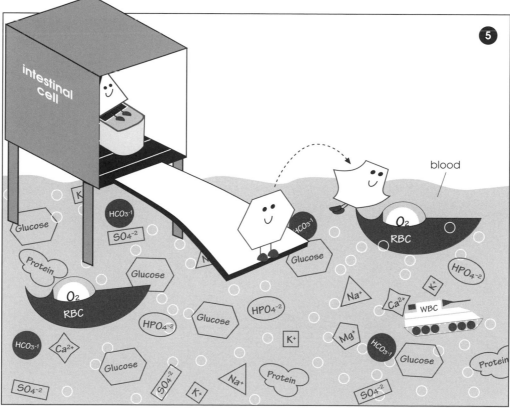

There are a number of factors that can hasten or slow the digestion of starch and thus the absorption of glucose into the bloodstream. Some of these factors are the nature of the starch, how it is prepared and cooked, and whether or not other nutrients are eaten with it, such as protein or fat. Each nutrient is digested and absorbed at a different rate. Eating other nutrients along with starches will slow the rate at which glucose enters the blood. The most significant factor, however, is the total amount of carbohydrate (in grams) that is eaten in a given meal.

Insulin Production
from Pancreatic Beta Cells

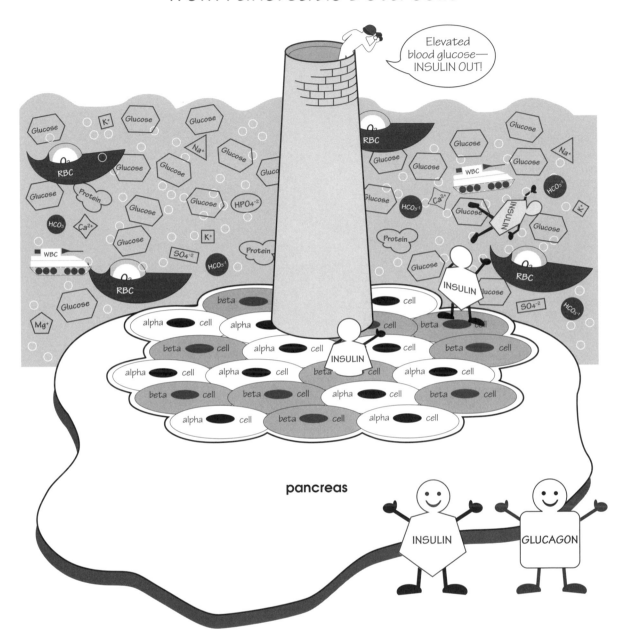

pancreas

The human nervous system works around the clock. Because it relies upon glucose as its primary fuel source, blood glucose concentrations are carefully maintained within a narrow acceptable range. It is neither safe for the blood to be overloaded with glucose nor for it to have too little glucose.

When carbohydrate-containing foods are eaten, they are digested and absorbed; thus, their component glucose molecules enter the blood from cells in the small intestine. Two groups of specialized cells of the pancreas monitor glucose levels. As glucose comes into the blood, pancreatic beta cells release the hormone insulin. The quantity released is directly related to the quantity of glucose that enters the blood. Following its release, the job of insulin is to travel in the blood and bind to specially-shaped receptors on cells that use insulin and to help bring glucose inside.

Glucagon Production
from Pancreatic Alpha Cells

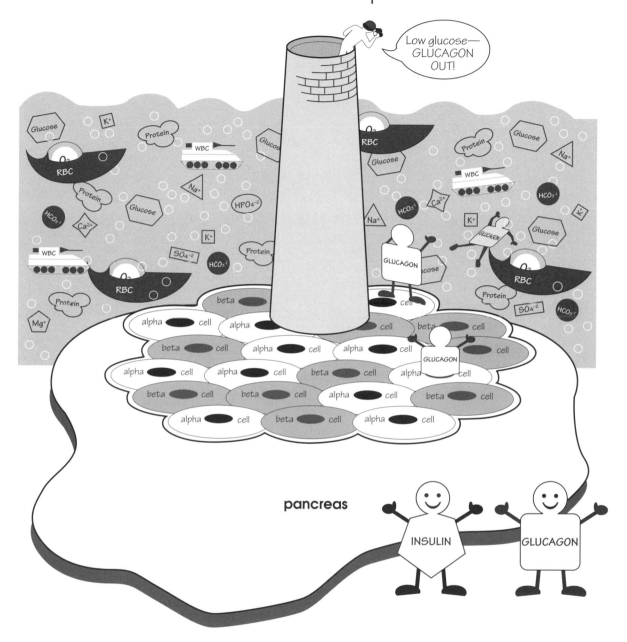

Blood glucose levels rise and fall as a result of the balance between our intake of carbohydrate-containing foods and body cells' uptake of glucose. Additionally, the liver can store and release glucose into the blood during time periods when we haven't eaten. It can store enough glucose to last for several hours. However, once its reserves are depleted, we must eat carbohydrate-containing foods.

When glucose levels fall too low, another group of specialized pancreatic cells, the alpha cells, respond. They release the hormone glucagon, which works along with a number of other hormones, including epinephrine produced by the adrenal gland, to cause the liver to release its glucose reserves into the blood. This is how glucose balance is restored in the absence of a meal.

Glucose Entry into Cells

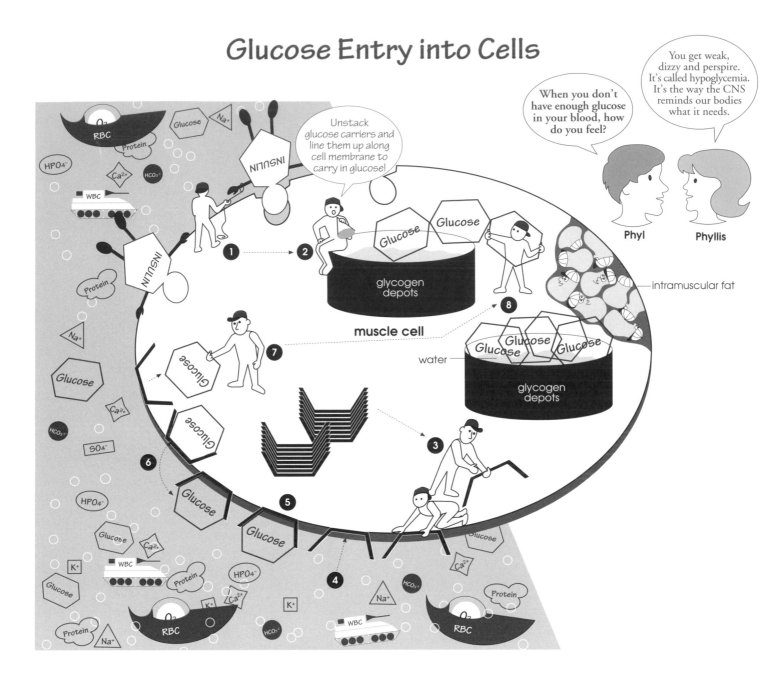

After digestion and absorption, glucose molecules that enter the blood travel in its fluid, the plasma, to muscle, liver, and other body cells that use it. In body cells that require insulin for glucose uptake such as muscle cells, insulin binds to specially-shaped receptors on those cells. This binding initiates a step-by-step process that ultimately carries glucose inside cells, where it is used immediately or stored for later use.

Glucose is stored as hundreds or thousands of glucose molecules stranded together in a form called glycogen. Glycogen is stored in special depots in water, and when needed it is once again broken down into its component glucose molecules. In muscle cells, glucose is used to make ATP to fuel work.

While liver cells do not directly require insulin to carry glucose inside, they do, in fact, store glucose as glycogen. As you have already learned, the liver serves as an important reserve to maintain glucose balance when we haven't eaten for a number of hours or while we are exercising.

Use of Glucose in the Muscle Cell during Exercise

MCS - Muscle Contractile Service

Oh, insulin levels are very low during exercise because glucose is needed to make ATP and is not stored as glycogen. Insulin promotes storage of fuels.

Phyl

When the body is exercising, the adrenal gland secretes the hormones epinephrine and norepinephrine into the blood to facilitate greater oxygen transport to working muscles. Epinephrine also promotes mobilization of our body's stored fat and liver glycogen. During exercise, blood levels of insulin are very low so muscle cells tend to use glucose to make ATP for muscular work rather than store glucose as glycogen. Muscle cells also use fat as fuel to make ATP, provided there is adequate oxygen. Mobilization of liver glycogen helps to maintain normal blood glucose levels during exercise.

Yes, and it appears that a mechanism in the muscle contractile process works during exercise instead of insulin to bring additional glucose into muscle cells.

Phyllis

Fat Conversion from Excess Calories

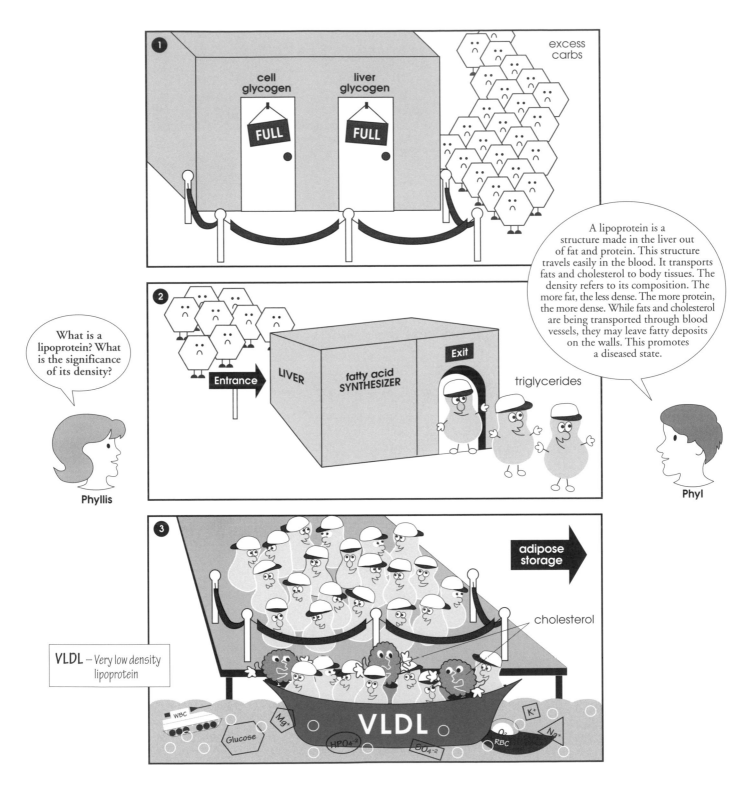

Carbohydrates are an important fuel source. They are eaten, digested, and absorbed. Then they are used or stored as glycogen. Once all of the glycogen depots have been filled, excess carbohydrate taken into the body—regardless of the healthiness of its source—will be converted in the liver to fat and sent out into the blood to the body's fat storage areas. Fat may be taken into the body from dietary sources or made in the liver from excess carbohydrate.

Fat Conversion from Excess Calories

LDL - Low density lipoprotein
LPL - Lipoprotein lipase

fat cells

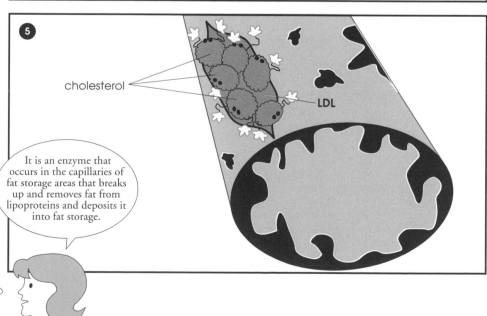

What is the pancreas?
Why is it important?
What is glucose balance?
What is insulin resistance?
What is metabolic syndrome?

Phyl and Phyllis's Physiology Phorum

Every cell in the human body performs work using the energy obtained from ATP. ATP is made from energy-yielding nutrients that are contained in the foods we eat. Nutrients are digested, absorbed, transported, and delivered to cells, where they are used immediately or stored. The use or storage of body fuels is under the influence of a complex organ called the pancreas.

The pancreas is composed of a variety of specialized groups of cells. Among these are the pancreatic acini cells, the alpha cells, and the beta cells. Each group of cells manufactures and secretes different substances.

The pancreatic acini cells manufacture and secrete digestive enzymes. These enzymes are released into the small intestine. Different enzymes are designed to break each of the chemical bonds specific to carbohydrates, fats, and proteins. Pancreatic acini cells also release bicarbonate, which neutralizes the acidic contents entering the small intestine from the stomach.

The alpha and beta cells manufacture and secrete the hormones glucagon and insulin, respectively. Secretion of either of these hormones, working with other hormones in the body, regulates the concentration of nutrients in the blood. Because the human nervous system preferentially uses glucose for its function, the regulation of blood glucose is particularly important. Working around the clock, the brain requires glucose even as we sleep. Glucose balance is therefore carefully maintained. Neither high levels (hyperglycemia) nor low levels (hypoglycemia) are desirable, and therefore, glucose concentrations are kept within a narrow, acceptable range.

After a meal, nutrients enter the blood from intestinal cells. Plasma, the fluid of the blood, provides the transport medium. Vitamins, minerals, blood cells, oxygen, carbon dioxide, and blood proteins all travel in the blood plasma along with energy-yielding nutrients, glucose, fat, and amino acids. The rate of transport and delivery of nutrients depends on the demands of cells.

As the nutrient concentrations rise, pancreatic beta cells secrete insulin. Insulin travels in the blood to appropriate cells where working with other hormones, it promotes nutrient uptake and storage.

Glucose is stored in body cells in the form of glycogen. The glycogen stored inside muscle cells is broken down into glucose to make ATP when it is needed for work. The glycogen that is stored in the liver serves as a glucose reservoir when concentrations of glucose in the blood fall too low.

Fat, the body's most abundant fuel supply, is stored in fat cells. Small amounts of fat are also stored inside of muscle cells. Fat makes large quantities of ATP.

The amino acids derived from protein food sources are primarily used to build and repair body tissues and other important materials. There is a small "pool" of amino acids always available in the body. If not required for energy, they are typically stored within the body's tissues and structures.

Insulin is the body's most important fuel storage hormone. Its actions are so important that anything that interferes with its work in the body will likely result in the development of disease. If insulin production by the beta cells is in any way impaired or if body cells that use insulin do not respond as they should to it, the resulting condition is appropriately called "insulin resistance." Insulin resistance can promote a cascade of events that can have devastating consequences. Cardiovascular diseases and diabetes mellitus are diseases that are the result of interference with the work of insulin.

The risk of developing insulin resistance is increased by a number of factors. While some factors are genetic, an individual is at far greater risk from physical inactivity, overeating, and the resulting

obesity. Abdominal obesity, in particular, is one of the first indicators that disease processes may have already begun.

Waist circumference measurements (at the level of the umbilicus) of greater than 35 inches in women and 40 inches in men are considered significant clinical indicators of insulin resistance syndrome, also known as metabolic syndrome. A growing waistline is obvious enough when it becomes difficult to button a pair of pants that once fastened easily. Other conditions that typically occur in metabolic syndrome are not as obvious without additional measurements and testing.

Higher than normal blood glucose concentrations (hyperglycemia), elevated blood pressures (hypertension), and abnormal blood fat concentrations (dyslipidemia) are common characteristics of metabolic syndrome. For those individuals with a family history of diabetes, screening through various tests and measurements should be part of a routine physical examination. Blood glucose measurement is important. Higher than normal blood glucose test results may be a message that metabolic disease is in progress. Thus, in order to prevent the development of diabetes, lifestyle change becomes necessary.

National Cholesterol Education Program (NCEP)

According to NCEP guidelines, metabolic syndrome exists if three or more of these traits are present:

- Abdominal obesity: a measurement of waist circumference (at the level of the umbilicus) greater than 35 inches for women or 40 inches for men

- Triglyceride measurement of 150 milligrams per deciliter (mg/dL) or higher

- Blood pressure measurement of 130/85 millimeters of mercury or higher

- A fasting blood glucose measurement of 110 mg/dL or higher

- A measurement of high-density lipoprotein cholesterol – the "good" cholesterol – lower than 50 mg/dL for women or 40 mg/dL for men

The Pancreas

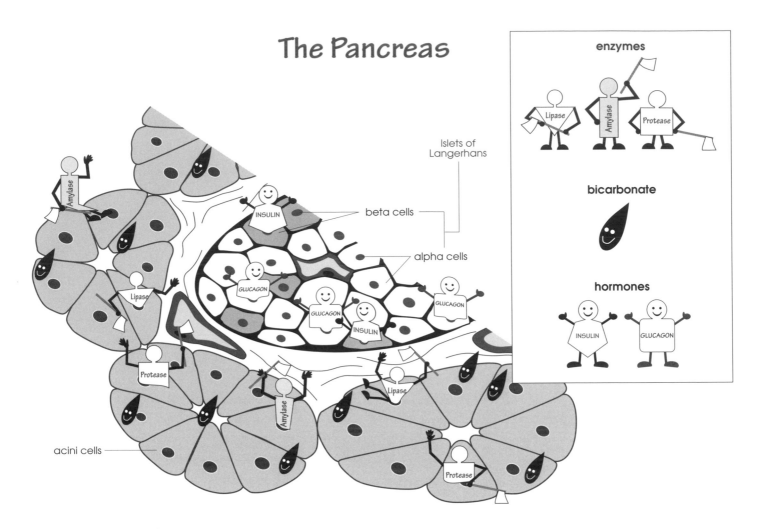

Islets of Langerhans

beta cells

alpha cells

acini cells

enzymes

Lipase
Amylase
Protease

bicarbonate

hormones

INSULIN
GLUCAGON

While blood glucose levels are maintained in a narrow acceptable range, they also fluctuate under a number of different circumstances. While the majority of this discussion pertains to hyperglycemia, blood glucose levels may, in fact, fall too low. Low blood glucose, called hypoglycemia, causes symptoms such as light-headedness, shakiness, fatigue, and sometimes a feeling of disorientation. These symptoms are the body's way of alerting us that something is wrong. The human nervous system protects itself in this way. When we are hypoglycemic, the body's stress response is activated. The adrenal glands produce epinephrine and norepinephrine, which cause a multitude of actions aimed at correcting a threatening situation. In this case, the nervous system thinks that the body is starving.

Epinephrine immediately turns off the beta cells' production of insulin because fuel storage is not desirable at this time. Instead, fuel must be released from reservoirs to raise the concentration of blood glucose. Pancreatic alpha cells are activated and secrete the hormone glucagon. Liver cells respond to glucagon and circulating adrenal hormones, breaking down their glycogen and spilling their reservoir of glucose into the blood.

In the absence of insulin, amino acid uptake and protein construction are halted. Amino acids travel to the liver, where they are converted into glucose molecules and released into the blood. This process is called gluconeogenesis. Lack of insulin also halts the fat storage process. Epinephrine causes the release of fatty acids from fat storage.

Fatty acids travel to the liver where they are chopped into small units and packaged as acetoacidic acid. This package is also known as a ketone. Ketones are released by the liver and sent into the blood to be presented to cells as an alternate fuel source to make ATP, since blood glucose must now be preserved.

The actions of the adrenal hormones, glucagon, and other hormones raise blood glucose levels to correct or reverse hypoglycemia at times when food is unavailable. A carbohydrate snack or meal can act quickly to correct the situation.

Hyperglycemia

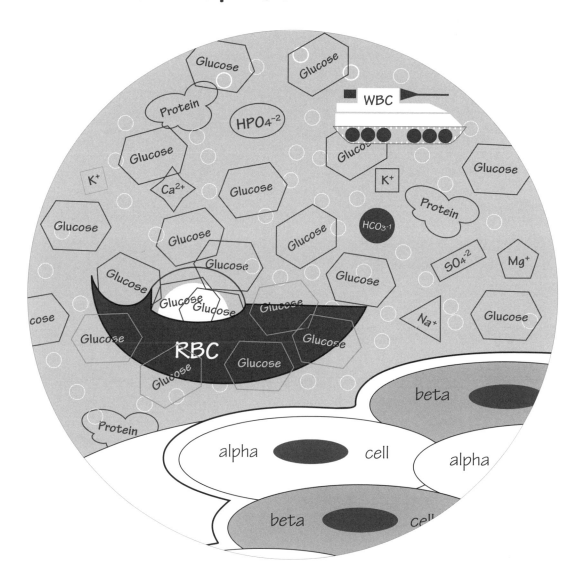

What if the glucose molecules could not be brought into our cells even if we ate a carbohydrate snack? What would happen if the pancreatic cells could not produce insulin? What would happen if the beta cells did produce insulin, but not as quickly as it was needed? What if insulin was produced, but when it got to the cell, it didn't work?

These scenarios describe diabetes mellitus, a group of diseases in which glucose molecules cannot be removed adequately from the blood plasma and taken up by cells. The resulting condition, hyperglycemia, leads to numerous other problems that interfere with all of the body's nutrient storage processes.

Imagine the blood plasma, with all of its constituents, transporting excessive concentrations of glucose. The concentrations are so high that our red blood cells start to look like sugar-dipped candies. Imagine all of the cells in the body that are insulin-dependent being unable to bring the glucose inside. They are starving for nutrients to make ATP to fuel their work.

How would I know if I had diabetes?

Is there more than one type of diabetes?

Phyl and Phyllis's Physiology Phorum

There are two broad classifications of diabetes mellitus: type 1 and type 2. Type 1 diabetes accounts for about 10 percent of the cases of diabetes; type 2 diabetes accounts for the other 90 percent. The less common, type 1, is an insulin-dependent diabetes, which typically begins in childhood. Type 2 diabetes typically occurs later in life, but has been recently

diagnosed in young individuals including teens and children in some populations. It tends to run in families and is often coincidental with obesity, particularly abdominal obesity.

In type 1 diabetes, the beta cells of the pancreas do not function. They are unable to produce any insulin. One possible explanation for their malfunction is that the body was exposed to a chemical or infection that caused the body's immune system to make antibodies. Not only did the antibodies attack the infection or chemical, but in the process, they also destroyed the beta cells.

In order to maintain glucose balance without functioning beta cells, insulin must be obtained from an outside source. Patients with type 1 diabetes dose themselves with insulin in a regimen that mimics pancreatic insulin production as closely as possible.

The treatment of type 2 diabetes may or may not require the use of insulin to restore and maintain glucose balance. In type 2 diabetes, pancreatic beta cells may produce some insulin, but the production may be delayed or inadequate. It also may be that the insulin receptors in body cells don't respond as they should.

Type 1 Diabetes

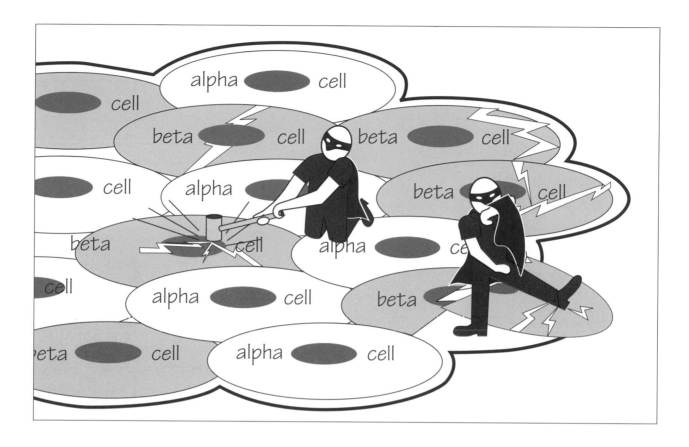

Type 1 diabetes may present suddenly. Type 2 diabetes typically develops gradually. During the disease progression from the early stages (pre-diabetes) to the diagnosis of type 2 diabetes, elevated blood glucose levels and insulin resistance may result in undetected yet significant damage to the heart, kidneys, eyes, nerves, and blood vessels. Screening for pre-diabetes is therefore highly recommended for a number of individuals, including those with family history of the disease or those who possess other characteristics associated with metabolic syndrome.

Pre-diabetes may be detected by a variety of different tests. A fasting blood glucose measurement is fast, reliable, and convenient. In a fasting glucose measurement, blood is drawn after a fast of at least eight hours. The concentration of glucose is measured relative to a deciliter (dL) or one tenth of a liter of blood. Concentrations of between 110mg/dL and 125mg/dL are indicative of impaired fasting glucose or pre-diabetes. Concentrations of greater than 126mg/dL indicate diabetes.

If the results of the fasting glucose test indicate pre-diabetes, an oral glucose tolerance test is the next step. An oral glucose tolerance test monitors glucose uptake by cells over a designated period of time. First, a fasting glucose measurement is taken. Then the patient drinks a glucose beverage. Blood is drawn at regular intervals. Normally functioning beta cells should produce enough insulin and cells should be able to respond appropriately so that glucose is removed from the blood at a specified rate. That rate should correspond to normal blood glucose concentrations for each designated time period.

A normal two-hour glucose measurement should be less than 140 mg/dL. Concentrations between 140 mg/dL and 199mg/dL are indicative of impaired glucose tolerance or pre-diabetes. Concentrations above 200 mg/dL are indicative of type 2 diabetes.

Insulin Resistance → Metabolic Syndrome → Type 2 Diabetes

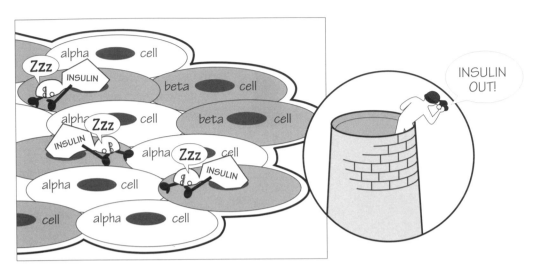

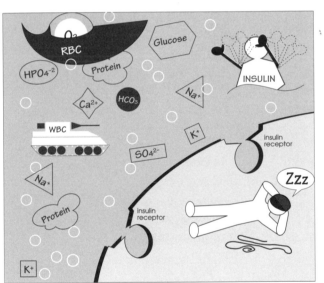

Previously referred to as "adult-onset diabetes," type 2 diabetes was a disease of middle-aged or older adults. Today, metabolic syndrome and type 2 diabetes are being diagnosed in more and more children, teens, and young adults. Along with a genetic predisposition, the primary controllable risk factors are physical inactivity and diets high in calories and saturated fat. An increase in physical activity and a healthier diet, along with other lifestyle changes, are recommended to treat and/or reverse metabolic syndrome and prevent type 2 diabetes. If lifestyle changes do not reverse symptoms of metabolic syndrome within three months, various medications are recommended to assist in treatment.

American Diabetes Association Parameters for Blood Glucose Tests

FASTING GLUCOSE TEST (FGT)

Fasting glucose measurement describes the concentration of glucose in milligrams dissolved in one tenth of a liter (one deciliter) of blood after an eight to twelve hour fast.

ORAL GLUCOSE TOLERANCE TEST (OGTT)

The oral glucose tolerance test measurement describes the concentration of glucose in milligrams dissolved in one tenth of a liter (one deciliter) of blood two hours after ingesting a glucose beverage.

1 deciliter

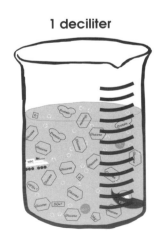

GLUCOSE MEASUREMENTS (mg-dL)

FGT	OGTT
Normal 80-110	Normal <140
Impaired Fasting Glucose 110-126	Impaired Glucose Tolerance 140-199
Diabetes ≥126	Diabetes ≥200

What are the symptoms of diabetes?

What are some of the resulting complications?

Phyl and Phyllis's Physiology Phorum

If glucose cannot be brought into cells and instead remains in high concentrations in the blood, body cells are deprived of an important fuel supply. Fatigue and other symptoms eventually become apparent. For example, hyperglycemia presents a challenge to the kidneys. Under normal circumstances, glucose molecules are filtered into the kidney tubules. Through a special transport system, glucose is reabsorbed at the kidney tubules and does not leave the body in the urine. Excessive glucose concentrations create a problem for the kidneys' reabsorption capacity.

As a result, glucose spills into the urine. The water in the kidney tubules follows the glucose out of the body. Hyperglycemia causes frequent urination. Cells become dehydrated. Excessive thirst results.

When cells resist insulin, all of the body's storage processes are reversed. Amino acid uptake and protein construction are halted. Muscles atrophy. Fatty acids are released rather than stored. Ketone concentration in the blood rises. Ketones are acidic and change the neutral environment of the blood. Excessive acidity from high concentrations of ketones is dangerous and may result in coma or death.

Hyperglycemia Challenges the Kidney

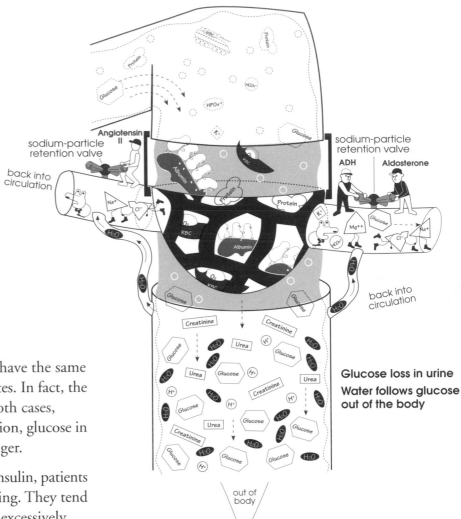

Glucose loss in urine
Water follows glucose out of the body

Patients with type 1 diabetes do not have the same difficulties as those with type 2 diabetes. In fact, the two are quite different diseases. In both cases, hyperglycemia causes excessive urination, glucose in the urine, fatigue, and increased hunger.

However, due to the total absence of insulin, patients with type 1 diabetes are literally starving. They tend to lose weight, even though they are excessively hungry and eat more. They also may have high concentrations of ketones in their blood, which is a condition called ketoacidosis.

Patients who develop or progress to the development of type 2 diabetes from metabolic syndrome, however, are typically obese. Many also have high blood pressure and are at a high risk of developing cardiovascular diseases. Most have some insulin activity, though it may be slow and not as effective as that in a healthy person. Ketoacidosis is not as common in a type 2 diabetic. Over time, patients with type 2 diabetes may develop blurred vision as a result of their eyes' chronic exposure to high concentrations of glucose.

Patients with either disease are at significant risk for the development of several complications if their glucose balance is not restored. Elevated blood glucose is associated with greater fat and cholesterol production in the liver, which promotes blood vessel damage, atherosclerosis, and high blood pressure.

Type 2 diabetics who are already obese increase their risk of heart disease if they do not lose weight. A five to ten percent loss of body weight has been shown to significantly improve one's overall health profile. The heart already struggles to pump blood through a disproportionately over-fat body. Diabetic complications make the situation even worse.

Small and large blood vessels throughout the body can be damaged by chronic exposure to hyperglycemia, elevated blood pressure, and high cholesterol. Tiny blood vessels of the eyes, the glomerulus of the kidney nephrons, and nerves can be damaged.

Wound healing may be delayed in diabetic patients. Damaged blood vessels limit blood flow to injured areas. Therefore, processes that would promote proper healing do not occur. Nerve damage may even prevent the sensation of an injury, so wounds are sometimes ignored until infections occur.

How is diabetes treated?

What are the recommended nutritional therapies?

How does exercise help to treat diabetes?

The primary goal in the treatment of diabetes is to restore and maintain glucose homeostasis or reverse hyperglycemia. Careful glucose control helps to prevent complications, such as damage to nerves, kidneys, eyes, and small blood vessels. Careful control means self blood glucose monitoring as well as a combination of nutritional therapy, increased physical activity and structured exercise, and medication, if necessary.

Blood glucose must be monitored several times daily as well as long-term. Many different blood testing kits are currently available. Typically, a finger is pricked and glucose is measured from a drop of blood. It may be measured upon waking, before meals, and before and after exercise. Physicians, along with certified diabetes educators, can help plan an appropriate protocol for each individual patient.

Overall glucose control can be monitored every few months through the administration of a long-term test called a glycosylated hemoglobin test. It is also called an HbA1c test. This test measures the amount of glucose attached to the oxygen-binding protein, hemoglobin, in red blood cells.

Self-Monitoring of Blood Glucose

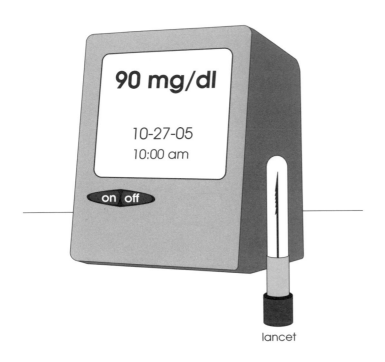

90 mg/dl

10-27-05

10:00 am

on off

lancet

Red blood cells are made in the bone marrow and have a typical life span of about 120 days. Glucose is used for the red blood cell's work during its life span. Though small amounts of glucose may be bound to hemoglobin, there should not be an abundance of glucose. However, if hyperglycemia has not been controlled over the life span of the red blood cell, a high percentage of the hemoglobin is bound with excessive glucose. Thus, the results of the HbA1c test indicate higher than normal numbers.

Measurement of Long-Term Glucose Control

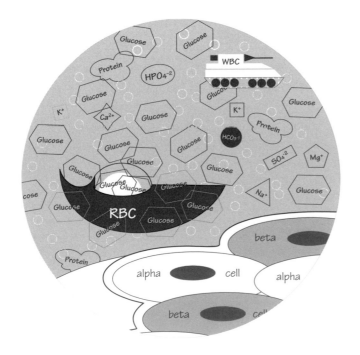

HbA1c Percentages	Level of Control
> 10-14	Poor
9-10	Marginal
7-9	Good
5-7	Goal

List of Food Groups
and Exchanges

Food Category / Portion	Carbohydrate	Protein	Fat		Total Calories
Carbohydrates					
Whole Grains and Starchy Foods 1 slice bread, 1/3 c. rice or pasta, 1/2 c. cereal	15g	3g	0-1g		80
Vegetables – 1/2 c. cooked, 1 c. raw veggies	5g	2g	—		25
Fruits – 1 4-oz. apple, 1/3 melon, 1/2 c. of juice, 1 61/2 -oz. orange	15g	—	—		60
Milk – 1 c. milk, 1 c. yogurt	12g	8g	Low-fat ....5g Whole................8g		120 150
Meats and Meat Substitutes 1-oz. meat	—	7g	Very lean..........0-1g Lean ....3g Medium-fat ....5g High-fat 8g		35 55 75 100
Healthy Fat – 2 tsp. peanut butter, 1 tsp. oil (canola, olive or peanut), 1/8 avocado, 10 olives, 6 almonds or cashews, 10 peanuts	—	—	5g		45

As diabetes research moves forward, new information and discoveries lead to modification of strategies for treatment and prevention. Thus, the American Diabetes Association's (ADA) recommendations for nutritional therapies are continually revised. As guidelines change, patients must be properly advised and educated.

The ADA recommends nutritional therapy that leads to the achievement of individual and general goals for all diabetic patients. Individual goals depend on several factors including age, size, activity level, lifestyle, food preferences, medication regimens and necessary calorie control. General goals are aimed at restoring normal metabolic function. This can be accomplished by following dietary strategies that help to: restore and maintain glucose control so that diabetes complications can be minimized; normalize and maintain blood lipids to prevent further development of cardiovascular diseases; and reduce blood pressure to prevent further damage to blood vessels.

Currently, the ADA does not recommend or endorse a specific diet. Nor does it recommend percentages of the macronutrients (carbohydrates, fats and protein) in the diet. Rather, diabetic patients are urged to eat a wide variety of foods from the three major food groups listed in the ADA Exchange Lists. The lists provide excellent nutritional guidance for both diabetic and non-diabetic individuals.

The lists divide foods into three groups: carbohydrates, which include whole grains and starchy foods, fruits, vegetables and milk; meats and meat substitutes; and fats. Portion size is designated for each group. Each portion of the food group is called an exchange. An exchange has a uniform constitution. It also has similar nutrients and approximately the same caloric value.

While they do not specify percentages of macronutrients, the ADA suggests that a healthy diet consist of a minimum of the following: three servings of nonstarchy vegetables; two servings of fruit; six servings of whole grains, beans or starchy vegetables; two servings of low-fat or fat-free milk products; and approximately six ounces of meat or meat substitutes. Fat and sugar are allowed, albeit in small

Approximate Number of Portions
Based on Calories

Food Group	1200 Calories	1500 Calories	1800 Calories	2000 Calories	2500 Calories	2900 Calories	3200 Calories
Carbohydrates							
Whole Grains and Starchy Foods 80 Kcals/serving	4	6	8	10	12	14	16
Vegetables 25 Kcals/serving	3	3	4	4	5	6	6
Fruit 60 Kcals/serving	3	3	4	4	5	6	6
Milk/Yogurt 90-120 Kcals/serving	2	2-3	2-3	3	3	3	3
Meats and Meat Substitutes	4-6	5-7	5-7	6-8	7-9	9-10	10-12
Healthy Fats 45 Kcals/serving	4	5	7	8	9	11	12

quantities. The actual numbers of servings of each type of food will vary and depend on total daily calorie requirements and other individual goals.

Foods listed in the carbohydrate group are nutrient-dense, which means that they provide several important nutrients in each serving. For example, whole grains, fruits, and vegetables provide glucose, protein, vitamins, minerals, and both soluble and insoluble fiber, all of which promote good health and also provide energy to fuel activity. Soluble fiber, such as that contained in oat bran, barley, nuts, seeds, beans, citrus fruits, apples, and numerous vegetables, has been shown to lower blood lipids. Insoluble fiber, such as that contained in whole grains, vegetables, and wheat bran, has been shown to aid in digestive health. In addition to carbohydrates, milk products contain the protein and calcium needed for maintaining healthy body tissues, bones, and teeth, while aiding in several important physiological processes.

The ADA neither recommends a particular percentage of carbohydrate in the diet, nor specific foods from which they should come. However, for the best glucose control and prevention of diabetes complications, it is recommended that each meal contain a consistent quantity (in grams) of nutrient-dense carbohydrates. Also suggested is a total daily quantity (in grams) of carbohydrate, which will depend on individual needs.

Fats are an important nutrient for diabetes nutritional therapy in terms of restoring and maintaining a normal blood lipid profile. Some fats are described as healthy or unhealthy depending on the risk they pose for the development of cardiovascular diseases. Their saturation is what deems them either dangerous or conducive to good health. Saturation refers to the chemical structure of a fat.

Saturated fats, which are found in foods from both animal and some plant sources, increase bad cholesterol. This presents serious problems for diabetics who already have compromised metabolic function. In addition to saturated fats that naturally occur in foods, commercially packaged foods such as baked goods or margarine, contain trans-fatty acids, which are fats that are artificially saturated in order to prevent spoilage. These fats present a more serious threat in promoting cardiovascular diseases than saturated fats in animal foods. The ADA recommends a limit of saturated fat in the diet of between seven and ten percent, depending on an individual's metabolic profile.

Not all fats promote cardiovascular disease. Monounsaturated fats contained in foods like fish, nuts, olives, olive oils, seeds, and some polyunsaturated fats contained in vegetable oils, have been shown to improve blood lipid profile. The ADA recommends that these fats replace saturated fats in the diet, limiting the total dietary intake of saturated fats to a range between seven and ten percent, depending on an individual's metabolic function.

While healthy fats are important in the diet, it should be noted that all fats are calorie-dense, meaning that gram for gram they contain more than twice the calories of carbohydrates or protein. The ADA urges diabetic patients whose goals are calorie control and weight loss to be aware of the portion sizes and calorie values of all fats.

Protein is an important nutrient for diabetics. In a healthy body, amino acids, the building blocks of proteins, make up body tissues and structures. However, in a body that has difficulty using and storing glucose, tissues may be broken down and their component amino acids may be used as an alternate energy supply. Some diabetic patients may therefore require extra protein in their diets. High-quality protein food sources are egg whites, poultry, fish, lean meats, beans and lentils. It is important to note that some diabetics may have kidney disease and thus may be directed by their physicians to limit protein intake.

Lowering blood pressure is an important goal in the treatment of many diabetics, who often struggle with hypertension. One way blood pressure can be lowered is weight loss. Another is by eating fresh foods that are low in sodium. Processed or canned foods are often preserved by chemicals that contain sodium. Food labels should be read carefully to determine sodium content. Recommended maximum sodium intakes will vary, however as little as 200 to 300 milligrams may be recommended for individuals with high blood pressure.

While general goals for diabetic nutrition therapy are aimed at restoring normal metabolic function, type 1 and type 2 diabetes are quite different diseases. For the type 1 diabetic who relies completely upon an outside source of insulin to use and store glucose and other nutrients, glucose control is primary and all else is planned around it. For the type 2 diabetic, who may still have some insulin production, albeit impaired, weight loss helps to improve glucose control and overall metabolic function.

For the typically obese type 2 diabetic, calorie control is a primary strategy. Creating low-calorie, low-fat, high-fiber, low-sodium, nutrient-dense, filling meals requires education, planning, guidance, and support. Other lifestyle changes including increased physical activity and structured daily exercise are equally important. The combined effects of adherence to both will hopefully result in weight loss and improved metabolic function.

Type 1 diabetes typically occurs in childhood, when growth is not yet complete. Because the type 1 diabetic relies entirely upon insulin for glucose control, insulin therapy is carefully directed. Insulin levels must closely imitate normal pancreatic beta cell function. Baseline insulin levels are maintained through long-acting types of insulin. Blood levels of insulin are maintained after meals by faster-acting insulin. Children are taught how to self-administer insulin either through injections or insulin pumps.

For type 1 diabetics, meals must be eaten in a manner that best maintains even glucose levels. Frequent small, nutrient-dense, carbohydrate-consistent meals are recommended to accomplish this. In addition to maintaining even glucose levels, it is important for the type 1 diabetic to eat sufficient calories to support a healthy body weight, carefully considering growth and activity levels. It is also imperative that glucose be carefully self-monitored with regard to meal planning and participation in physical activity, structured exercise, and sports.

Exercise Helps Control Hyperglycemia

The American Council on Exercise and American College of Sports Medicine recommend three to five days per week of moderate cardiovascular activity and at least two days a week of progressive resistance training for maintenance of healthy bone and muscle tissue in apparently health individuals. Exercise is particularly important for the diabetic.

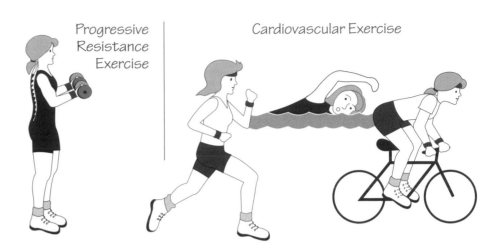

Progressive Resistance Exercise

Cardiovascular Exercise

For type 1 diabetics, three to five days of low to moderate cardiovascular exercise such as walking, jogging, or biking for twenty to thirty minutes is suggested. With a physician's approval, two to three days of standard progressive resistance training followed by appropriate stretching is suggested, provided there are no limiting complications.

Type 2 diabetics lose weight best with daily low to moderate cardiovascular exercise that accumulates to achieve forty to sixty minutes of work. This can be accomplished during the course of the day in single or multiple bouts of exercise. Two days of progressive resistance training is recommended, using low resistance and high repetitions. This program is best suited for the overweight, hypertensive diabetic who already may have atherosclerosis. The choices of activities and programs are subject to any limiting complications and a physician's approval.

In addition to daily activities, exercise uses calories and reduces fat storage, thus helping to reverse insulin resistance. For both types of diabetics, exercise improves heart and lung function and therefore blood flow. Exercise also helps to maintain a strong and healthy musculoskeletal system.

Exercise also helps to control hyperglycemia by bringing glucose into muscle cells without insulin. During exercise, even under normal circumstances, adrenal hormones turn off insulin production by beta cells. They also cause the breakdown and release of fuels. This is because during exercise, fuel is needed to make ATP so that muscles may perform their work.

During the muscular contractile process, another system of glucose transport into cells is activated – one that does not require insulin. Moderate exercise, therefore, can remove a substantial amount of glucose from the blood. Additionally, for several hours after exercise, glucose uptake is increased.

For type 1 diabetics, exercise may mean fewer doses of insulin. However, with exercise, close monitoring of blood glucose levels and proper timing of meals is imperative. Insulin dosage must be adjusted to avoid hypoglycemia. Carbohydrate snacks must be available to counteract hypoglycemia.

For type 2 diabetics, exercise can mean lower doses of medication or perhaps, after a time, no medication. Type 2 diabetics sometimes require medication and sometimes do not. Their medications target such insulin resistance problems as delayed beta cell response, lowered numbers of insulin receptors, or poorly functioning insulin receptors. A program of proper nutrition and exercise may result in weight loss that contributes to significantly improved glucose balance.

The proper combination of diet, exercise, medication, and close monitoring can help maintain glucose balance in diabetics so that they may live normal, healthy lives, free of serious long-term complications. Regular eye examinations, kidney-function testing, blood lipid profiles, and blood-pressure monitoring are essential. Good hygiene and monitoring the extremities for wounds and infections are important as well.

Essential Nutrients

Chapter 6
Fats

Roles and Forms of Fat

Roles

Good Roles of Fat

1. Energy
2. Cell Membranes
3. Hormone Structure
4. Organ Protection
5. Satiety
6. Immune Function

Also known as lipids, fats are a group of chemical compounds found throughout the body as integral components of cell membranes, reproductive hormones, digestive materials, and nerves. Fats provide insulation and organ protection and assist in immune function and other responses to trauma. They are necessary for the transport and storage of fat-soluble vitamins. Dietary fats add flavor and aroma to foods and help create satiety, or a sense of fullness, during and after meals. The primary roles of fat, however, are to provide fuel and to store energy for the body's work.

Triglycerides

glycerol — fatty acid chains = Glycerol

The majority of stored body fat and most dietary fat takes the form of triglycerides. Triglycerides are made up of the same structural elements as carbohydrates—carbon, hydrogen, and oxygen atoms—but in different numbers and proportions. Triglycerides consist of a molecule of glycerol attached to three carbon chains of varying length. The carbon chains are called fatty acids.

Chemical Structures of Fat

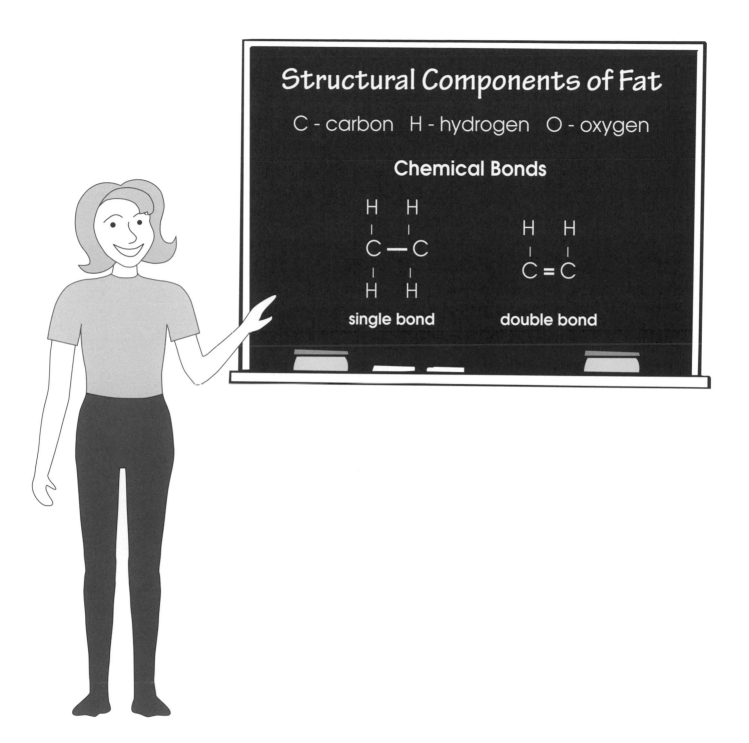

Most fatty acids that the body needs can be assembled in the liver. However, there are two families of fatty acids that cannot be assembled in the liver and therefore must be eaten in foods. Called essential fatty acids, these important fats are the omega-6 and omega-3 fatty acids. Omega-6 fatty acids, also known as linoleic acid, are found in the oils of grains and seeds. Omega-3 fatty acids, also known as alpha-linoleic acid, are found in green leaves and seeds. Omega-3 fatty acids can also be constructed from the fatty acids contained in fish.

Chemical Structures of Fat

Linoleic Acid

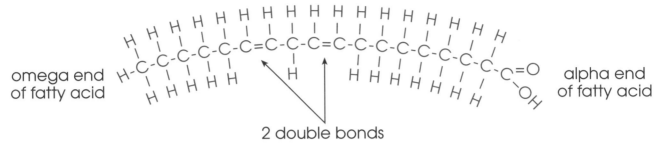

omega end of fatty acid

alpha end of fatty acid

2 double bonds

Sources

Rich sources of omega-6 fatty acids are corn, safflower, soybean, and sunflower oils.

Alpha-Linoleic Acid

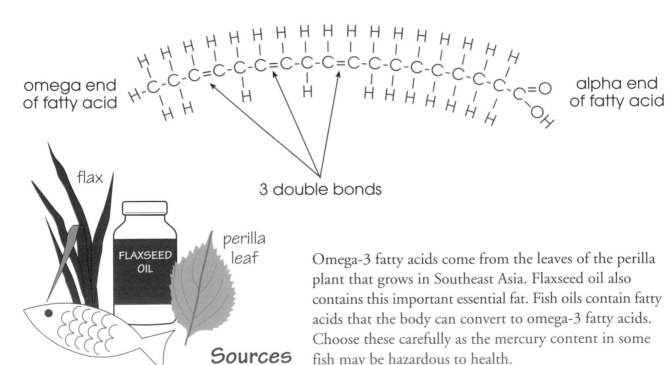

omega end of fatty acid

alpha end of fatty acid

3 double bonds

flax

perilla leaf

Sources

Omega-3 fatty acids come from the leaves of the perilla plant that grows in Southeast Asia. Flaxseed oil also contains this important essential fat. Fish oils contain fatty acids that the body can convert to omega-3 fatty acids. Choose these carefully as the mercury content in some fish may be hazardous to health.

Chemical Structures of Fat

Saturated Fatty Acids

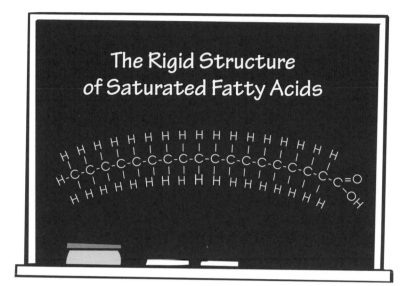

Fatty acids are categorized according to the length of their chains and degree of saturation. The length determines the type of fatty acid. The degree of saturation refers to the chemical arrangement, which in turn determines whether the fat is hard or soft at room temperature.

If every carbon atom along a fatty acid chain bonds to its maximum number of hydrogen atoms, the fatty acid is saturated. Because of its chemical structure, saturated fatty acids remain solid at room temperature.

Saturated fatty acids occur naturally in such animal foods as pork, beef, fish, and dairy products as well as such plant foods as palm and coconut oils. While they occur naturally, fatty acids can also be saturated during food processing in order to extend shelf life. Food companies can chemically alter the unsaturated fatty acids in their products through a process called hydrogenation. During this process, hydrogen atoms are added to the unsaturated fatty acids in such foods as margarine, shortening, commercial baked goods, and pastries. The resulting synthetic fats are called trans-fats.

Trans-Fats

Nutrition Facts	
Serving Size	1cup (228g)
Servings Per Container	2

Amount Per Serving	
Calories 250	Calories from Fat 110

Total Fat	12g
Saturated Fat	3g
Trans Fat	3g
Cholesterol	30mg
Sodium	470mg

While hydrogenation may prevent spoilage in products in grocery stores, trans-fats present problems inside the human body. Current research shows that the greater the consumption of trans-fats, the higher the risk for development of type 2 diabetes, cardiovascular, and other diseases. Thus, the Food and Drug Administration has mandated that nutrition facts labels on foods must reveal the trans-fat content. In fact, since studies have revealed that many saturated fats present a significant health risk, the current United States Department of Agriculture (USDA) Guidelines recommend their consumption be limited to ten percent or less of one's total diet.

Chemical Structures of Fat
Unsaturated Fats

Monounsaturated

1 double bond

Polyunsaturated

2 double bonds

While every carbon atom along a saturated fatty acid chain bonds with its maximum number of hydrogen atoms, making it straight and rigid, the chemical configurations of unsaturated fatty acids are different. Their carbon chains have one or more locations where instead, two adjacent carbon atoms form a double bond. This allows the structure to bend, thus be fluid at room temperature.

If such a double bond occurs at only one location, the fatty acid is monounsaturated; if at more than one location, it is polyunsaturated. Consumption of monounsaturated fats, found in such foods as olive oil, canola oil, peanut and almond oils, pecans, and avocados has been associated with a reduced risk for disease. Polyunsaturated fats, found in such foods as corn, safflower, soybean, and sunflower oils contain important essential fatty acids.

While the makeup of fatty acids may seem inconsequential, eating foods containing unsaturated rather than saturated fatty acids has important health benefits. The content and quality of the foods we eat become the materials used to build our body's structures. Additionally, the chemical arrangements of foods can significantly influence the function of body cells.

For example, cell membranes with a more fluid constitution respond to and interact better with chemical messengers. Chemical messengers tell cells, and therefore tissues, what to do. Thus, body processes run more smoothly and efficiently with more fluid cell membranes made from unsaturated fatty acids. For these and several other health reasons, dietary fats should be carefully chosen.

Fat Digestion and Absorption

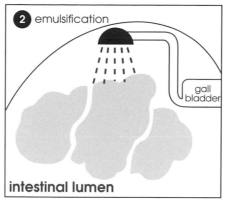 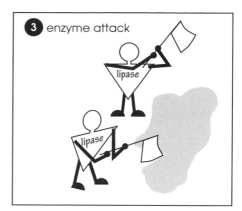

  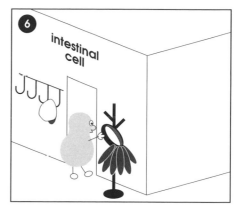

 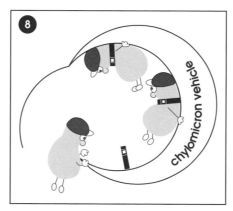 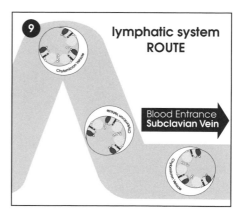

The fats that we eat are digested and absorbed at the small intestine in a relatively complex and time-consuming way. The stomach must empty slowly when fat is being digested. We therefore stay full longer when fat is in the stomach.

The stomach empties fat into the small intestine. It is emulsified or broken into small globules in the intestinal lumen by bile from the gall bladder. Pancreatic enzymes called lipases break up the globules and form triglycerides. Triglycerides arrive at the intestinal cells in a form called a micelle. Triglycerides travel in the body in a carrier called a chylomicron. Chylomicrons are too large to enter the blood at the small intestine. Therefore, they take an indirect route via the body's lymphatic system.

Fatty Acid Entry into Adipose Storage

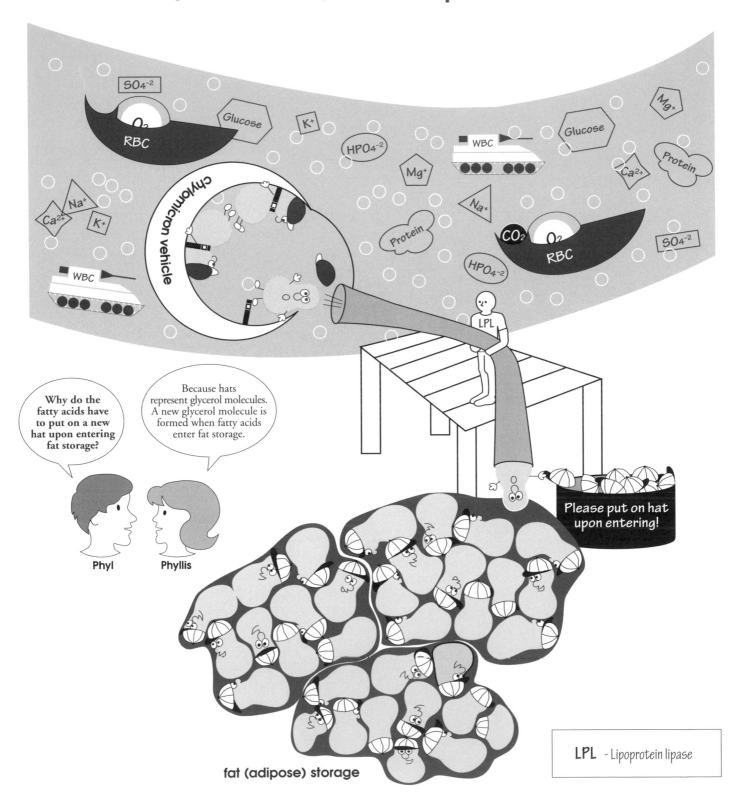

fat (adipose) storage

LPL - Lipoprotein lipase

Once fat has made its way into the bloodstream, it is quickly taken out of the blood and deposited into fat-storage areas throughout the body.

Release of Fatty Acids from Adipose Storage

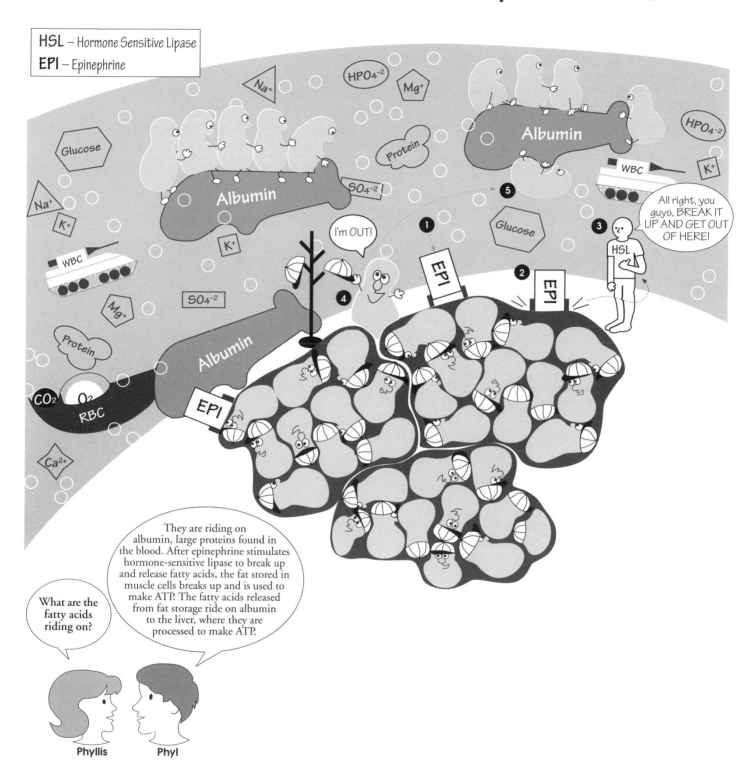

Fat, like carbohydrate, is an important fuel source. In fact, fat is the most abundant fuel source in the body. Glycogen storage in the liver and muscles is limited. Fat storage, on the other hand, is virtually unlimited. While you sit and read this book more than half of your body's fuel to make ATP will come from fat. When the body is exercising, epinephrine circulates throughout the body and causes release of fatty acids from fat-storage areas. If working muscles receive adequate oxygen, released fat will be used to make large amounts of ATP.

Beta Oxidation:
Fatty Acid Breakdown and Formation of Acetoacetic Acid

When fatty acids are released from storage, they travel in the blood via albumin protein carriers to the liver. In the liver, they are chopped into units and packaged in a form that the muscles can use to make ATP. In order to use fat, muscles need plenty of oxygen as well as adequate carbohydrate. Carbohydrate breakdown materials are necessary in order to use fat as a fuel.

Fat Calories Add Up Quickly

Fats are important to several physiological functions and provide numerous health benefits. However, it is important to remember that fats yield nine calories per gram. While the fatty acids in nut butters may yield health benefits, a tablespoon is almost 200 calories and need not be eaten with a spoon directly from the jar. Salads that are drenched in oily dressings are not "diet" meals. Foods that are fried would be healthier and lower in calories if baked.

Calories from fat can add up quickly. Excess consumption of fat, or any nutrient in the diet, not only leads to an unattractive appearance, it challenges the body throughout daily life. An over-fat body is difficult to move. Both the joints and the heart are overstressed. Breathing is difficult. The pancreas struggles to provide adequate insulin; cells become resistant to insulin. The current USDA Dietary Guidelines recommend that even healthy fats do not exceed 35 percent of the total daily calories. Moderate calorie and fat intake coupled with daily exercise helps to utilize fat stores and prevent excessive fat gain.

What is atherosclerosis?

What is cholesterol?

What are lipoproteins?

What determines whether cholesterol is "good" or "bad"?

Phyl and Phyllis's Physiology Phorum

Atherosclerosis is one of the two most common cardiovascular disorders; the other is high blood pressure or hypertension. Atherosclerosis is characterized by numerous lumps or plaques occurring within and throughout the walls of large and medium sized arteries. The most commonly affected arteries are the coronary arteries that serve heart muscle tissue and the carotid arteries that serve brain tissue.

Plaques begin to develop as a result of damage to the protective endothelial layer of cells that line the inner wall of arteries. The damage may be the result of chronic exposure to high blood pressure. It may also occur as a result of chronic exposure to high concentrations of "bad" cholesterol, also known as low-density lipoproteins.

Atherosclerosis tends to run in families. However, there are such controllable risk factors as smoking, diets high in saturated fat and cholesterol, physical inactivity and the resulting obesity.

Cholesterol

Low-Density Lipoprotein

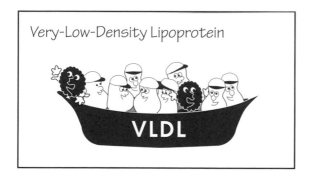

Very-Low-Density Lipoprotein

High-Density Lipoprotein

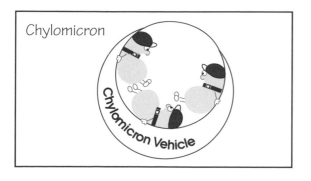

Chylomicron

Although the disease process begins in childhood, it may not be detected until young adulthood. Because family history is an important predictor of cardiovascular disease, its manifestations should not be dismissed in childhood. Blood pressure measurement and examination of blood components should be a routine part of pediatric care.

Cholesterol is a fatty, waxy substance either brought into the body through the diet or made from fat inside the liver. Among other roles in the body, cholesterol serves as an important component of reproductive hormones and digestive materials. It is also an integral part of cell membranes.

As is the case with all lipids, or fatty substances, cholesterol is transported aboard protein structures to and from cells that use it. These carriers are called lipoproteins, the density of which depends upon what is being transported. There are several lipoproteins of varying density. Three of the most important are: very-low-density lipoproteins (VLDLs), low-density lipoproteins (LDLs) and high-density lipoproteins (HDLs).

Very-low-density lipoproteins (VLDLs) are constructed in the liver. They transport triglycerides and cholesterol to fat storage areas throughout the body. After the triglycerides are removed, the lipoprotein increases in density and becomes a low-density lipoprotein (LDL). LDLs are sometimes called "bad" cholesterol because of the risk they pose if they are trapped within blood vessel walls and go through a process called oxidation. Oxidized LDLs tend to form plaques associated with the development of atherosclerosis.

High-density lipoproteins (HDLs) are also constructed in the liver. They travel through the body collecting the excess cholesterol from arterial walls. Then they carry it back to the liver. HDLs are known as "good" cholesterol because their removal of cholesterol from arterial walls reduces the risk of the development of atherosclerosis. Chylomicrons are also carriers of fat, transporting the triglycerides contained in foods to fat storage areas.

Lipid Profile

Date Reported	Date Received	Patient Name - I.D.	Phone	Age	Sex
08-AUG-05	07-AUG-05	Phyllis Physiology	312-386-2782	45	F

Date Collected	Time Collected	Hospital I.D.	Requisition No.	Assession No.
07-AUG-05	8:30 am		361586829	2555006782-5

Client Name/Address		Test Requested
Lake Shore Cardiologist Chicago, IL	27570-4 [7]	Metabolic Panel, Comprehensive Lipid Panel Thyroid Panel with TSH.

Physician	Volume	Fasting	Patient SS#	Comments
Bergin, C		Yes		Copy sent to patient

TEST NAME	RESULT	UNITS	REFERENCE RANGE
Lipid Panel:			
Cholesterol	191	MG/DL	100-199
Triglycerides	110	MG/DL	20-199
HDL-Cholesterol	58	MG/DL	35-150
LDL (Calculated)	110	MG/DL	0-129
VLDL (Calculated)	18	MG/DL	(39

While lipids are essential for a variety of cellular functions and therefore must be transported in the blood to and from the liver, the transport must be rapid. The concentration of blood lipids fluctuates, but is lowest after fasting, which is when blood should be drawn for a lipid profile.

A lipid profile is a routine blood test that can be administered during an annual physical examination. It is a measurement of the concentration of blood lipids (in milligrams) dissolved in a deciliter of blood after a twelve-hour fast.

Desirable results are high concentrations of HDLs (≥60mg/dL), and low concentrations of LDLs (100 mg/dL). Triglyceride values should ideally be as low as possible (150 mg/dL).

What is the relationship between LDL or "bad" cholesterol and the development of atherosclerosis?

How does this cause a heart attack or stroke?

Phyl and Phyllis's Physiology Phorum

The cells of healthy body tissues take up and use cholesterol for a variety of important functions. The remaining circulating LDLs must be removed from the blood. Both arterial endothelial cells and liver cells are equipped to remove them. The removal mechanism involves specially shaped proteins that are designed to bind with the LDL structure and remove its cholesterol.

While the primary mechanism provides effective cholesterol removal, chronically high concentrations of LDLs exhaust its ability to keep up. Thus, another mechanism is implemented—one that may be damaging to the protective endothelial lining of arterial walls. This alternative method of LDL removal involves a type of white blood cell called a monocyte, which changes into a macrophage. Macrophages gobble up excess LDL cholesterol.

Phyl and Phyllis's Physiology Phorum

Blood vessel walls that are continuously exposed to high concentrations of bad cholesterol must resort to calling in an army of macrophages to gobble up the excess LDLs. The removal process, however, disrupts the smooth cell-to-cell protective endothelial structure of the blood vessel walls. As with chronic high blood pressure, this disruption also allows the invasion of other blood constituents into vulnerable tissues beneath them. The damage to blood vessel walls caused by chronic high blood pressure and exposure to high concentrations of LDLs attracts blood cells called platelets to the areas of disrupted endothelium.

Platelets are important blood cells despite their small size. Platelets bunch together, or aggregate, when blood constituents or vessels are damaged. To control bleeding, they form a plug by releasing various sticky substances. The plug allows the body time to close up the wound. Platelet aggregation is an important process, but it sometimes occurs for no apparent reason. Fortunately, the body has safety mechanisms that dissolve unnecessary platelet aggregation or clotting.

When the protective endothelial layer is disrupted, platelets are attracted to the area of inflammation and damage. Platelets release substances that seem to cause abnormal tissue growth in these areas. The abnormal tissue growth, combined with the fatty materials gobbled up by the macrophages begins to form mounds that grow and harden into plaques. Atherosclerosis is the result.

Arteries in this condition are no longer stretchy and pliable. They no longer can accommodate the loads of blood the heart pumps into them. The piping system becomes rigid and narrowed, creating more resistance against which the heart has to pump. This raises blood pressure. Eventually, the affected arteries can become virtually blocked, impeding adequate blood flow, and therefore much needed oxygen and nutrients, to the heart muscle or brain tissue.

Plaque formation occurs throughout the cardiovascular system. Blood vessel walls that are hardened, bumpy and jagged like those affected by atherosclerosis are prone to cracking, promoting more platelet aggregation and clot formation. Should a clot attach to already existing plaques and get lodged in a small artery, it can block blood supply to heart muscle tissue, and cause a heart attack also known as a myocardial infarction. If a clot becomes lodged in an artery blocking blood supply to brain tissue, a stroke can result.

The Development of Atherosclerosis

1 Body cells, especially liver cells, possess special receptors that bind with LDL cholesterol and remove it from circulating blood. Once cells have taken up all they need, the LDLs that remain in the circulation are susceptible to attack by unstable substances. Thus, they may be chemically altered through a process called oxidation.

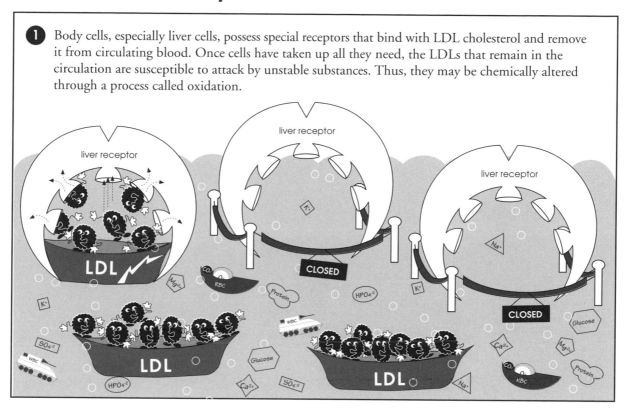

2 Oxidized LDLs are trapped by endothelial cells of blood vessel walls. White blood cells called monocytes are attracted to the area of entrapment.

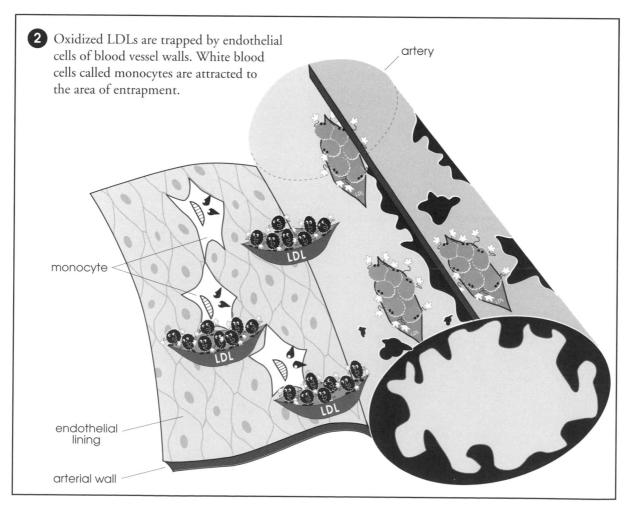

The Development of Atherosclerosis

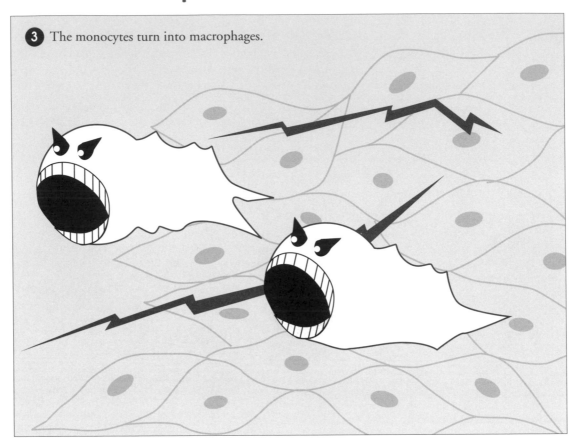

③ The monocytes turn into macrophages.

④ Macrophages gobble up the excess LDLs.

5 The damaged area of blood vessel endothelium becomes inflamed. Platelets clump together (aggregate) and rush to the inflamed area to plug up the damaged blood vessel wall.

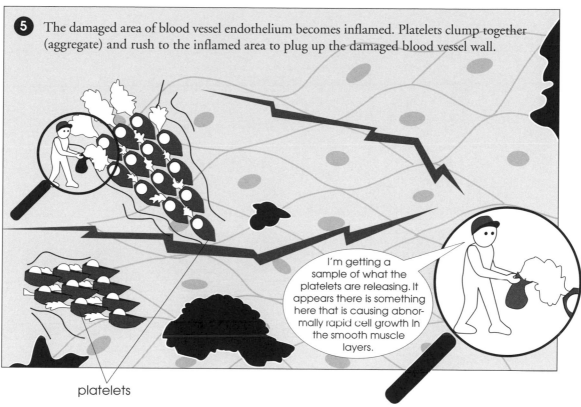

platelets

6 The platelets produce sticky substances that not only draw more platelets and other fatty components but also cause abnormal cell growth in the area. Hardened walls form mounds called atherosclerotic plaques.

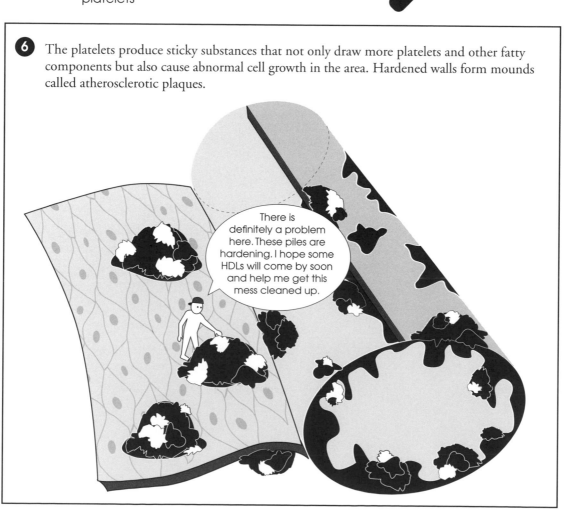

Essential Nutrients

Chapter 7
Proteins

Roles of Protein

1 muscle tissue

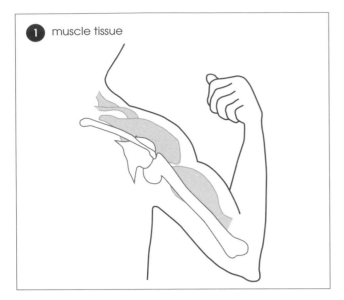

2 transportation vehicles

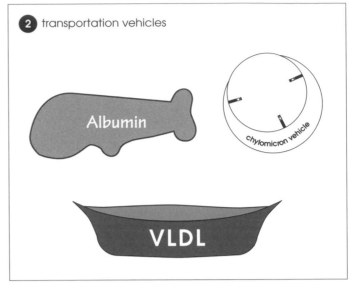

3 antibody and antigen

4 blood-clotting and scab-building

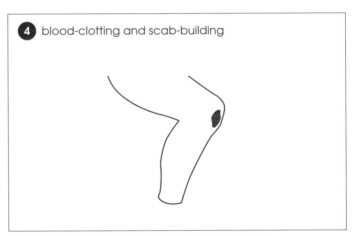

5 enzymes

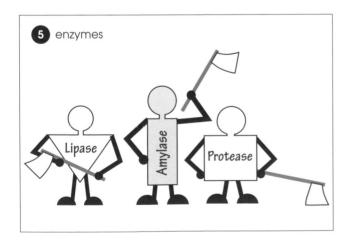

6 hormones

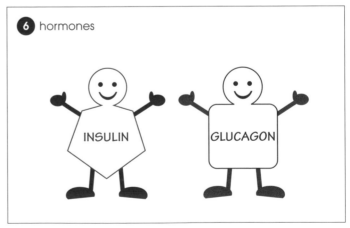

While carbohydrate and fat are important fuel sources for the human body, protein plays a different nutritional role. Protein is essential for the growth, repair, and maintenance of every tissue in the body. Many of the body's transportation vehicles and carriers are partially constructed of protein. Antibodies that kill germs are made of protein. Blood-clotting and scab-building materials are made of protein. Enzymes and some hormones are also made of protein.

Protein Construction Costs Energy

Proteins are constructed from several amino acids linked together by peptide bonds.
The energy supplied by fat and carbohydrate provide the ATP for protein construction.

Nine Essential Amino Acids

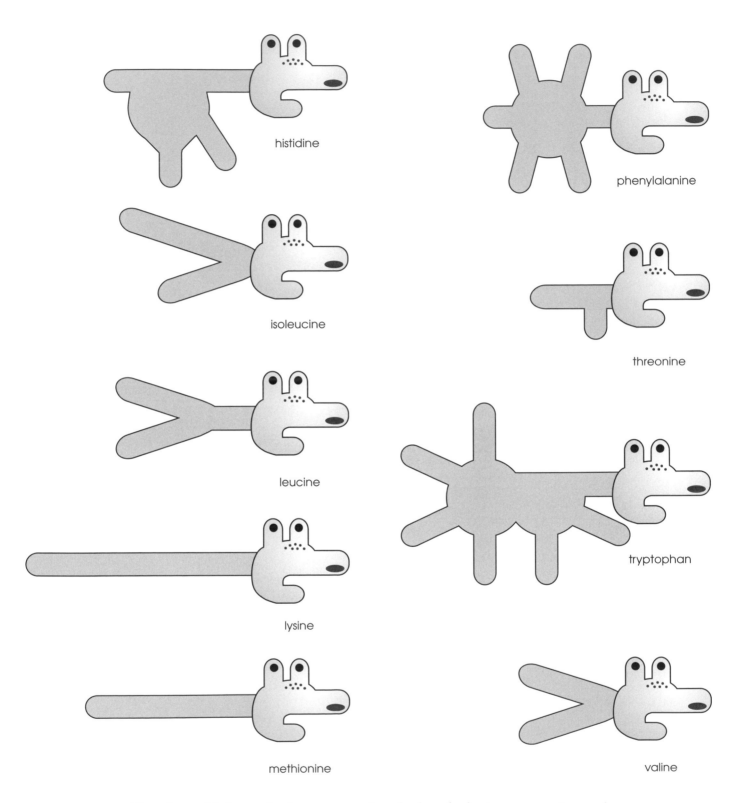

histidine

phenylalanine

isoleucine

threonine

leucine

lysine

tryptophan

methionine

valine

All amino acids have a basic structure. Attached to the basic structure is a variety of differently shaped chemical chains. There are twenty amino acids relevant to human nutrition. There are nine essential and eleven nonessential amino acids. The nine essential amino acids are histidine, isoleucine, leucine, lysine, methionine, phenylalanine, threonine, tryptophan, and valine.

Eleven Nonessential Amino Acids

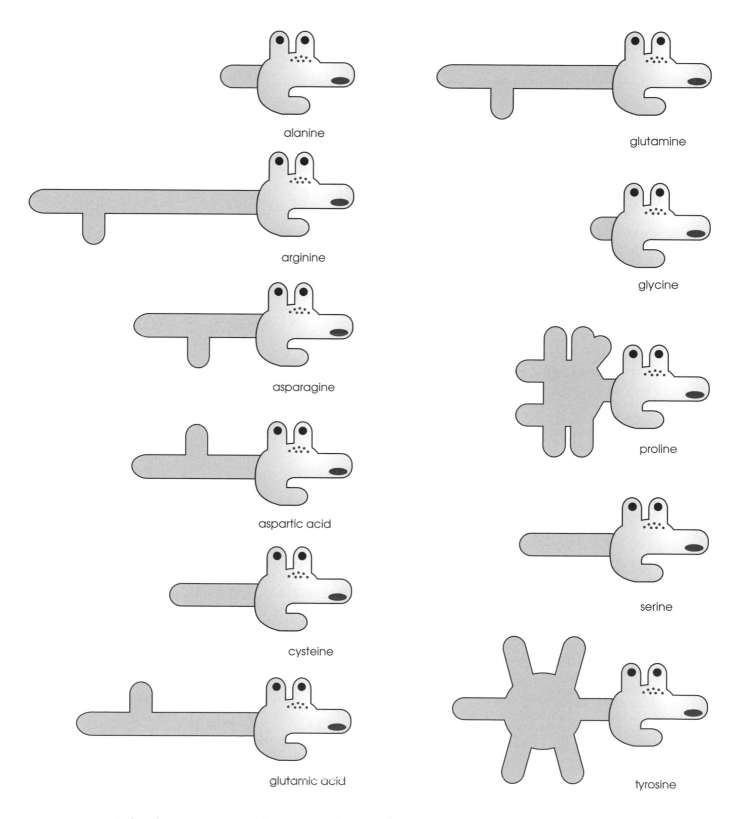

alanine

glutamine

arginine

glycine

asparagine

proline

aspartic acid

serine

cysteine

tyrosine

glutamic acid

The eleven nonessential amino acids typically can be manufactured as necessary for normal tissue repair and construction. The eleven nonessential amino acids are alanine, arginine, asparagine, aspartic acid, cysteine, glutamic acid, glutamine, glycine, proline, serine, and tyrosine.

Protein Construction

The exact sequence, shape, and character of all human protein is dictated by each individual's genetic instruction or DNA. In order to construct body protein, the diet should supply at least the nine essential amino acids in adequate amounts. Protein construction must be complete. Complete proteins contain all of the essential amino acids in relatively the same proportions as our body proteins.

Complete Protein
from Animal Sources

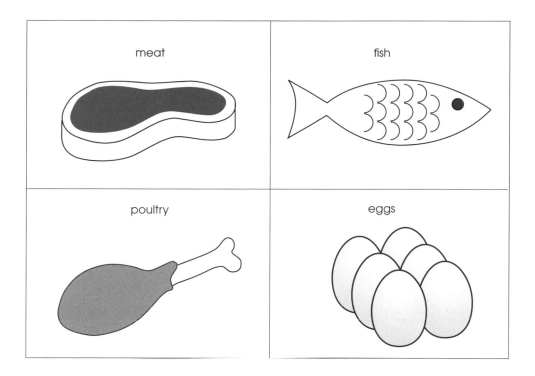

from Plant Sources

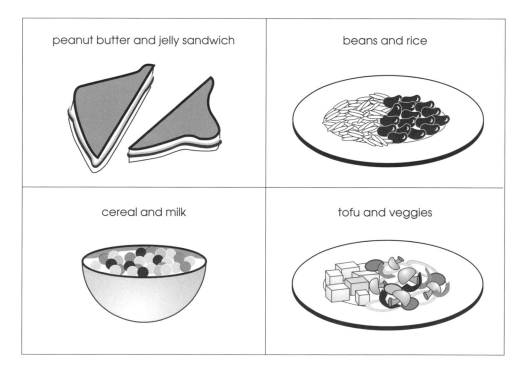

Good food sources for complete proteins are those from animal sources such as meat, fish, poultry, and eggs. However, carefully selected proper combinations of foods from plant and dairy sources may be adequate to make complete proteins.

Protein Digestion

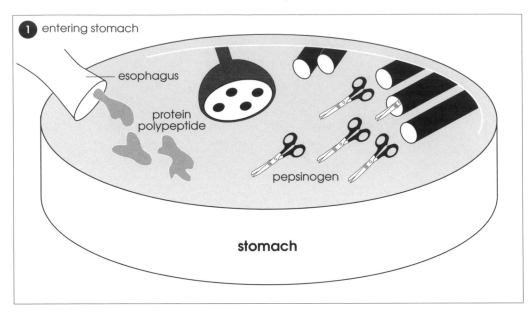

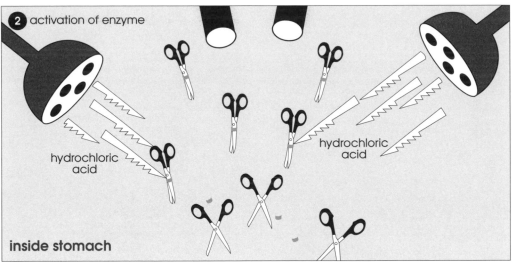

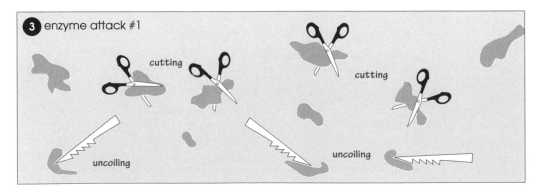

Protein digestion is a complex process. Protein enters the stomach from the esophagus. Specialized stomach cells secrete an inactive proteolytic enzyme called pepsinogen. Other stomach cells produce hydrochloric acid, which activates the pepsinogen and makes it into the active enzyme pepsin. This acid also changes the shape of proteins by uncoiling them so that pepsin can break the protein into smaller components.

Protein Digestion

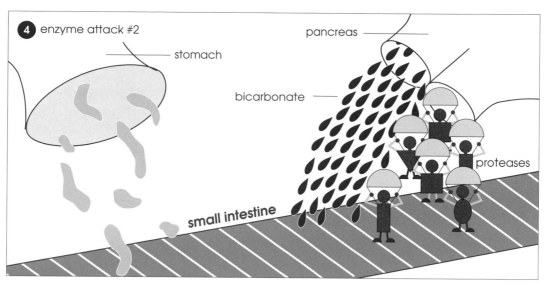

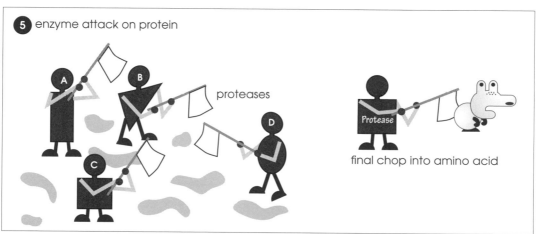

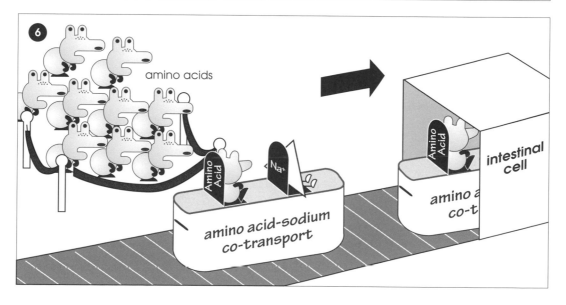

The broken-down protein enters the small intestine. The pancreas secretes two substances: bicarbonate, which neutralizes the acid, and digestive enzymes, which complete the process of protein digestion into amino acids.

Protein Absorption

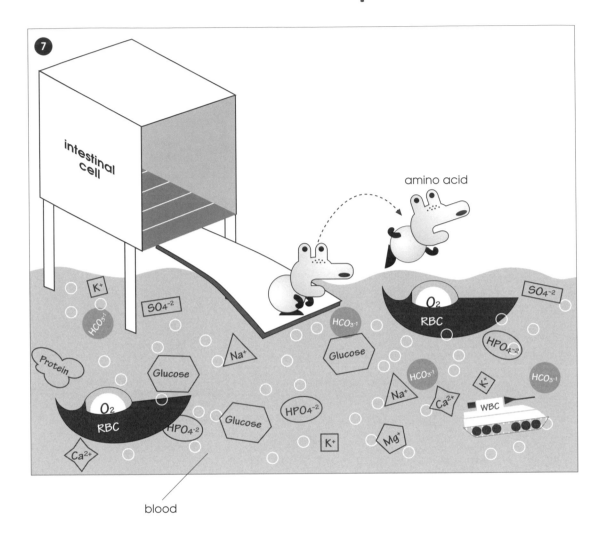

Amino acid absorption is similar to that of glucose.

Gluconeogenesis:
The Synthesis of Glucose from Amino Acids

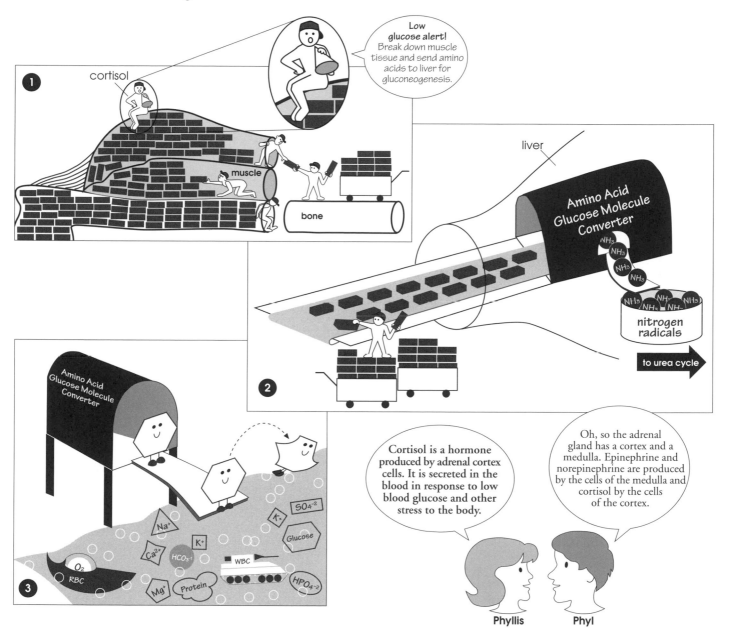

Unlike fat and carbohydrate, protein is infrequently used in the body as an energy source to make ATP. Only when the diet is lacking in carbohydrate is protein used in any appreciable amounts for energy.

When carbohydrate is lacking in the diet, the body's protein stores, for example, in muscle tissue, are broken down into their component amino acids. The amino acids are transformed in the liver into glucose molecules.

The glucose is then released into the blood so that the blood glucose levels remain adequate for use by the central nervous system. This process is called gluconeogenesis. Adequate carbohydrate in the diet ensures that the body tissues are not broken down to make fuel, but are used for the work for which they were constructed.

What are the factors that influence metabolic rate or the total daily energy expenditure (TDEE)?

Phyl and Phyllis's Physiology Phorum

The energy used to make ATP to fuel the body's work comes from nutrients contained in the foods we eat. The amount of energy available in nutrients is expressed in kilocalories, though we commonly refer to them simply as calories. One gram of carbohydrate or protein yields four calories. One gram of fat yields more than twice that, or nine calories. The rate at which the body's tissue cells use the calories to perform all of their work during the course of a day is called metabolic rate, also known as the total daily energy expenditure (TDEE).

There are three primary factors that influence the TDEE. These include: the resting metabolic rate (RMR), or the rate of energy expenditure that maintains basic life processes in the absence of activity; the thermic effect of food (TEF), which is the energy required to process foods; and activity, the energy required to fuel the body's physical work.

Kilocalories in Nutrients

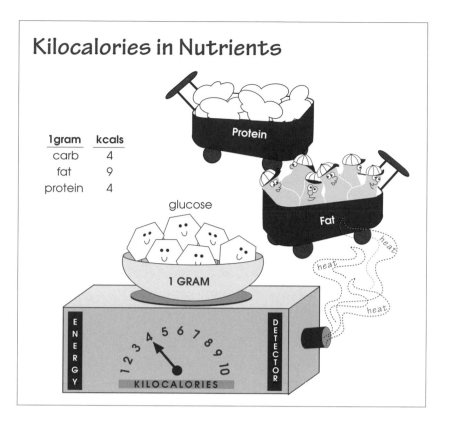

1 gram	kcals
carb	4
fat	9
protein	4

Resting Metabolic Rate (RMR)

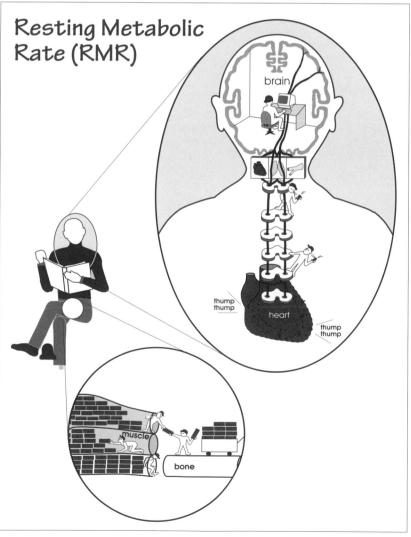

Even without physical activity, all of our metabolically active tissues require energy to function. During the course of a normal day, cells function like tiny factories. They build, break down and rebuild, package, secrete, and transport materials in and out. All of these processes require energy expenditure. Such energy expenditure is called the resting metabolic rate. RMR may be influenced by several interacting factors. These factors include an individual's body and frame size, body composition, (proportion of fat-free or muscle mass to fat mass), age, growth, gender, genetic predisposition, hormonal and nervous control, environmental temperature, illness, and medications.

Processing the nutrients in the foods we eat costs energy. Such energy expenditure is called the thermic effect of food. Foods are chewed, swallowed, and broken down through digestive processes. They are absorbed into the bloodstream and then transported to cells where they are used immediately or stored for later use. An individual may use ten percent of his or her total calorie intake to perform these processes. This means that for two thousand calories eaten during the course of a day, two hundred of those calories may account for the TEF.

Calorie Expenditures per hour of Common Activities*

ACTIVITY	CALORIES
Sitting quietly	84
Sitting and writing	114
Bicycling (5 mph)	174
Pacing (2 mph)	198
Dancing (ballroom)	210
Light housework	246
Volleyball	264
Swimming (20 yds/min)	288
Golf (carrying clubs)	324
Rollerblading/ice skating (9 mph)	384
Scrubbing floors	440
Basketball (recreational)	450
Tennis (singles, recreational)	450
Swimming (crawl, 45 yds/min)	522
Aerobic dancing	546
Bicycling (13 mph)	612
Jogging (6 mph/10 minute mile)	654
Cross-country skiing (5 mph)	690

Based on an individual who weighs 150 pounds or 68 kilograms

Daily physical activity level is the most controllable and significant factor in influencing metabolic rate or the total daily energy expenditure. Every cellular activity performed by the body costs energy. Physical activity costs a great deal more than sitting. For example, while you sit and read this book, you may use approximately one and a half calories per minute.

Yet, if you got up every hour and paced for five minutes, during that time, you could use three calories per minute. This notion is one to consider during the course of a busy day. A telephone conversation need not require that we sit, but in fact can be used to accomplish a mile of pacing during three calls lasting seven to nine minutes.

What is body composition?
How is it related to metabolic rate? Why is it so important to measure it?
How is it measured?

Phyl and Phyllis's Physiology Phorum

When we step onto a scale and see a number in pounds or kilograms, we do not see a calculation that tells us the composition of that body weight: the proportion of fat-free mass (FFM) to fat mass. Body composition describes this proportion and is a more accurate assessment of health than body weight. A high proportion of FFM and a healthy body fat percentage typically translate to a lower risk of cardiovascular and other diseases.

FFM includes organs, muscle tissue, nervous tissue, bones, blood components, connective tissues, and glands. All of these tissues are metabolically active. Though it has some important functions in the body, fat is not considered to be metabolically active. Metabolic rate is directly related to the quantity of FFM in an individual's body; the greater the FFM, the higher the metabolic rate.

Body Composition

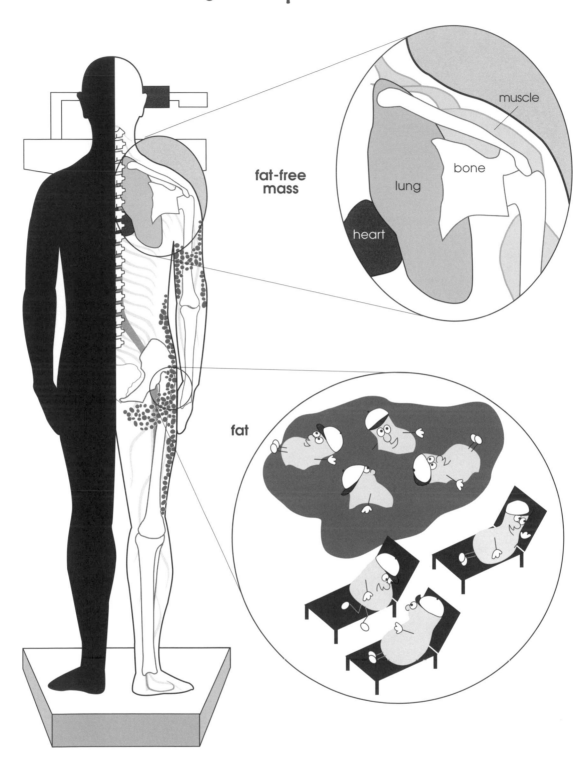

fat-free
mass

muscle

bone

lung

heart

fat

Due to the fact that body composition is a more accurate assessment of health than body weight, it is useful to measure the percentage of body fat. Attaining an exact measurement of body fat can be inconsistent and difficult. Traditionally, underwater weighing has been one of the most accurate methods of measuring body composition and body fat percentage. Underwater weighing estimates the density of the body tissues by weighing an individual on a special scale under water.

Today, this method is rarely available and has been replaced by another technique called Dual Energy X-Ray Absorptiometry (DEXA). Currently the "gold standard" method of measuring body composition, DEXA was originally used to measure bone mineral density. DEXA uses low energy x-rays and the known densities of fat, muscle, bone, and water to analyze the distribution and quantity of each throughout the body. Because abdominal obesity has been associated with the risk of the development of cardiovascular diseases and type 2 diabetes, it is useful to know body fat distribution as well as body fat percentage. DEXA can be costly, however, and it is typically only available in laboratory settings. Thus, other more affordable and accessible methods of measuring body composition may be utilized.

Bioelectrical impedance analysis (BIA), skinfold calipers, or anthropomorphic measurements, among other methods, may be used to estimate body composition. Bioelectrical impedance analysis (BIA) is an accurate, accessible, and painless method of estimating body fat percentage. In BIA, an individual is weighed; then height, age, gender, weight, and other information are entered into the computer of a BIA instrument. A small electrical current is then sent throughout the body and the resistance or impedance to it is measured.

Fat-free mass, much of which is muscle mass, contains a high proportion of water or fluid. Therefore, it imposes less resistance to the electrical current. Fat mass is composed of little water. Therefore, it presents greater impedance to the current. Body fat percentage is calculated by the BIA instrument based on the resistance or impedance a given body imposes on the circulating electrical current.

Another tool that is used to estimate body fat percentage is a skinfold caliper. The skinfold caliper measures pinches of skin with their underlying fat at designated sites. The sum of the measurements corresponds on a chart to an estimated body fat percentage.

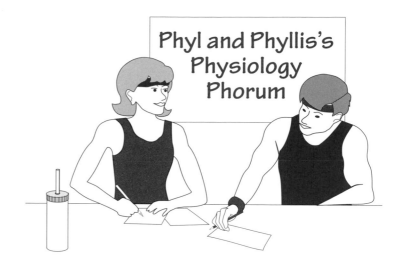

Phyl and Phyllis's Physiology Phorum

Anthropomorphic measurements estimate body composition by using a tape measure to measure designated sites. The measurements are placed in special equations. The result of the equation corresponds to an estimate of body fat percentage. One of the most simple and useful anthropomorphic measurements is that of waist circumference. Waist circumference of greater than 40 inches, or 102 cm, in men and 35 inches, or 88 cm, in women is considered a significant clinical indicator of metabolic disease and is associated with a high risk for the development of cardiovascular disease and type 2 diabetes.

Desirable body fat percentages depend on individual goals. For better performance, male athletes may desire five to seven percent body fat while female athletes are frequently estimated to be in the range of 12 to 15 percent. Eighteen percent to 23 percent body fat for adult women and 12 percent to 20 percent for adult men is considered optimal. Body fat in excess of 25 percent in men and 30 percent in women is considered over-fat. The term "over-fat" is used rather than overweight or obese because an apparently normal weight individual may possess an unhealthy body composition; a body with too little muscle and too much fat.

Body Mass Index (BMI)

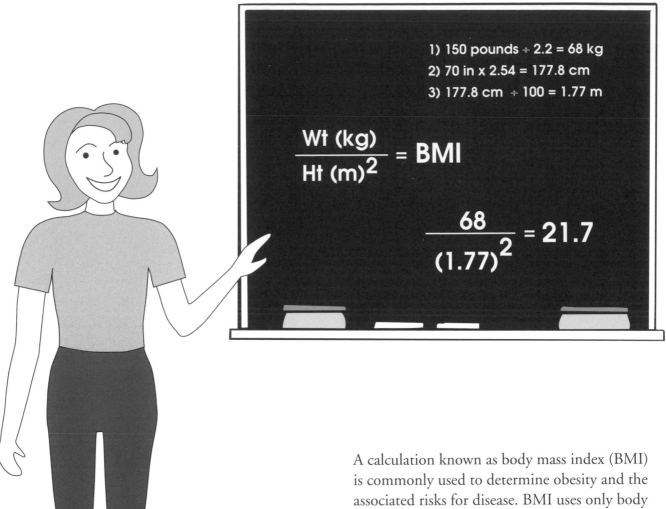

1) 150 pounds ÷ 2.2 = 68 kg
2) 70 in x 2.54 = 177.8 cm
3) 177.8 cm ÷ 100 = 1.77 m

$$\frac{Wt\ (kg)}{Ht\ (m)^2} = BMI$$

$$\frac{68}{(1.77)^2} = 21.7$$

A calculation known as body mass index (BMI) is commonly used to determine obesity and the associated risks for disease. BMI uses only body weight and height and does not factor in body composition. The calculation is made by dividing the body weight in kilograms by the height in meters squared. Numbers ranging from 18.5 to 24.9 are considered healthy and normal. Numbers ranging from 25 to 29.9 correspond to moderately overweight. Numbers greater than 30 correspond to obesity.

Like many methods, BMI has limitations. Alone, BMI numbers may not be representative of health risks for certain populations. For example, a muscular athlete may have so much muscle weight due to the density of his or her muscle that his or her BMI will be high. As previously discussed above, a "normal" weight, sedentary individual may have little muscle weight, a low BMI and still be over-fat.

What is energy balance?

What factors are important in maintaining energy balance?

What factors are important in weight loss and maintenance?

Phyl and Phyllis's Physiology Phorum

In order to maintain a particular body weight, one must maintain energy balance, which means spending all of the calories one eats over a given time period. During a twenty-four hour period, if fewer calories are eaten than are used, an energy deficit is created and weight is lost. Should weight loss be a goal, it is preferable that most of the loss be in body fat and not in fat-free mass (loss of muscle tissue would result in lowered metabolic rate). The healthiest and safest way to ensure this outcome is to reduce calories moderately while maintaining a sound nutrition program. It is also important to exercise and generally increase physical activity level.

Few people are aware of how much time they spend seated or sedentary during waking hours. Overall activity level plays an important role in maintaining a healthy body composition. Too frequently we skip meals, overeat or graze. We are unaware of portion sizes or the calories contained in the foods we eat. Important tools in weight loss and maintenance are avoiding hunger, determining portion size, maintaining calorie control, and keeping track of daily activity.

Hunger is a basic drive. Like any other animal, we are driven to eat when we are hungry. We will thus seek food in order to satisfy the hunger, without necessarily making healthy food choices. Hunger is strongest when we haven't eaten for a number of hours; the stomach is empty and blood levels of energy-yielding nutrients are low. This is especially true of blood glucose levels. After longer periods of time, the body's fuel supplies begin to run low. We tend to both overeat and make unhealthy food choices when hunger has reached this point.

✓ Do not skip meals; plan for times when meals will not be available during the course of a busy day; have healthy snacks accessible.

✓ Eat smaller, more frequent meals during the course of the day.

✓ Include a balance of carbohydrate, healthy fat and protein in all meals.

✓ Eat foods that fill—those that have volume, with the greatest amount of water content, fiber, and other nutrients and the least amount of calories.

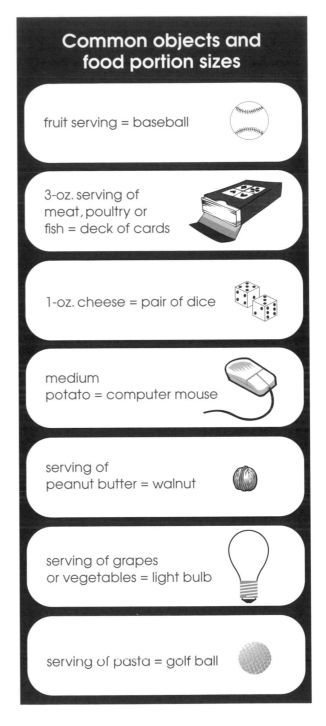

Common objects and food portion sizes

fruit serving = baseball

3-oz. serving of meat, poultry or fish = deck of cards

1-oz. cheese = pair of dice

medium potato = computer mouse

serving of peanut butter = walnut

serving of grapes or vegetables = light bulb

serving of pasta = golf ball

While it is unrealistic to bring measuring tools along during the course of a work or school day, it is important to be aware of the portion sizes and their associated calorie values for the different foods we eat.

One helpful way of avoiding extra calories is to recognize the portion sizes of different foods or food groups by associating them with common objects.

Becoming aware of your daily activity level is another way to observe and assess the healthiness of your lifestyle. Many of us spend countless hours sitting—behind desks working on computers, watching television, and eating meals. Getting up and moving often during the course of a day energizes us while it adds energy expenditure. There are numerous ways to spend energy and time other than seated.

What are the USDA Dietary Guidelines?

As with the American Dietetic and American Diabetes Association's Exchange system, the current United States Department of Agriculture's (USDA) Dietary Guidelines and accompanying Food Guide Pyramid provide a user-friendly food guidance system.

Among other valuable information, the guidelines offer suggestions for maintaining or achieving healthy body weight. Additionally, they provide key recommendations for calorie requirements, food groups, portion sizes, macronutrient balance, and weight management. They also address some of the important nutrient needs of special populations.

The guidelines encourage variety and nutrient density in the diet. Variety refers to the inclusion of several different kinds of foods, including vegetables, fruits, whole grains, lean meats or meat substitutes, healthy fat, and low-fat dairy food sources. Nutrient-dense foods are those that provide as many nutrients as possible within a given food portion. They also support meeting appropriate energy needs for activity level and lifestyle.

USDA Guidelines
General Recommendations

 Choose a wide variety of fiber-rich fruits and vegetables.

 Eat 2 cups of fruit and 2.5 cups of vegetables per day for a 2,000 calorie diet.

 Include dark green, orange, and colorful vegetables. Consume less than 10% of calories from saturated fatty acids; consume less than 300 mg of cholesterol.

 Keep total fat intake between 20 and 35%, coming mostly from sources of poly-unsaturated and mono-unsaturated fatty acids such as fish, nuts, and vegetable oils.

 Limit intake of fats and oils high in saturated and/or trans-fatty acids.

 Consume less than 2,300 mg of sodium per day.

 Limit alcohol consumption to 1 drink per day for women and 2 drinks per day for men.

USDA Key Recommendations

- To maintain body weight in a healthy range, balance calories from food and beverages with calories expended.

- To prevent gradual weight gain over time, make small decreases in food and beverage calories and increase physical activity.

For Specific Populations or Groups

- *Those who need to lose weight*
Aim for a slow, steady weight loss by decreasing calorie intake and increasing physical activity.

- *Overweight children*
Reduce the rate of body weight gain while allowing for growth and development. Consult a healthcare provider before placing a child on a weight-reducing diet.

- *Pregnant women*
Ensure appropriate weight gain as specified by a health care provider.

- *Breastfeeding women*
Moderate weight reduction is safe and does not compromise weight gain of a nursing infant.

- *Overweight adults and children with chronic diseases who may need medication*
Consult a healthcare provider about weight-loss strategies prior to starting a weight-reduction program to ensure appropriate management of other health conditions.

USDA Guidelines
Estimated Calorie Requirements
for Varying Lifestyles

AGE	*LIFESTYLE:	1. Sedentary	2. Moderately Active	3. Active
Males				
4-8		1400	1400 -1600	1600 - 2000
9-13		1800	1800 - 2200	2000 - 2600
14-18		2200	2400 - 2800	2800 - 3200
19-30		2400	2600 - 2800	3000
31-50		2200	2400 - 2600	2800 - 3000
51+		2000	2200 - 2400	2400 - 2800
Females				
4-8		1200	1400 - 1600	1400 - 1800
9-13		1600	1600 - 2000	1800 - 2200
14-18		1800	2000	2400
19-30		2000	2000 - 2200	2400
31-50		1800	2000	2200
51+		1600	1800	2000 - 2200

*Lifestyle Descriptions

1. Sedentary describes a lifestyle that includes tasks of daily living without additional activity.

2. Moderately active describes a lifestyle with activity such as walking 1.5-3.0 miles per day at 3.0 to 4.0 mph in addition to performing tasks of daily living.

3. Active describes a lifestyle with activity that includes walking more than three miles per day at 3.0 to 4.0 mph in addition to performing tasks of daily living.

The USDA Food Guide Pyramid is the product of a great deal of research, careful analysis, and interpretation of several food guidance systems. Each detail of the pyramid has a meaningful message. Each of the food groups is color-coded. Grains are coded as orange, vegetables as green, fruits as red, milks as blue, meats and beans as purple, and fats and oils as yellow. The recommended proportions of each food group are designated by the relative width of each colored band. The inclusion of physical activity recommendations, represented by a figure ascending stairs, is a new addition. The interactive web site at **www.mypyramid.gov** provides an abundance of user-friendly information and printable pages.

What is an energy deficit?

How is an energy deficit accomplished for healthy weight loss?

Phyl and Phyllis's Physiology Phorum

In order to lose body weight, an energy deficit must be created. This can be accomplished by increasing activity level and therefore increasing caloric expenditure and by moderately reducing caloric intake.

While caloric intake must be modified, it is important to eat enough calories in proper macronutrient proportions for optimal nervous system functioning. This will prevent significant loss of muscle mass. Without adequate intake of carbohydrates, the brain and nerves are deprived of glucose, their primary fuel source. As a result, metabolically active muscle tissue is broken down into component amino acids. Amino acids are converted in the liver to glucose. This process, called gluconeogenesis, helps maintain normal blood glucose levels at the expense of fat-free mass and metabolic rate.

USDA Acceptable Macronutrient Distribution Ranges

MACRONUTRIENT	RANGE

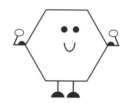

carbohydrate...........45% to 65%

fat ....20% to 35%

protein......................10% to 35%

A good part of an energy deficit should be created through increased physical activity and exercise. Exercise programs should combine cardiovascular exercise with progressive resistance training. The exercise program helps to utilize and potentially diminish fat stores. The progressive resistance training also helps to maintain muscle mass.

If an individual is already participating in a cardiovascular program, the program should be modified to create larger calorie deficit. The frequency, duration, and intensity of training can all be adjusted to increase calorie expenditure. Introducing new types of activities, cross training, or interval training (adding frequent one- to two-minute increments of higher intensity work) can be an enjoyable and effective way to use more calories.

What is progressive resistance training?

Why should it be added to the exercise program during weight loss?

Phyl and Phyllis's Physiology Phorum

Appropriate calorie consumption combined with progressive resistance training will help to maintain or minimize loss of muscle mass during weight loss. With weight loss of more than ten to fifteen pounds, it is difficult to avoid some loss of muscle mass. The desired result of a good weight management program is a reduction primarily of fat. This results in improved body composition.

Progressive resistance training is an exercise program that results in greater muscular strength and endurance. It is a program in which the intensity and the volume of exercise are increased gradually over time. Intensity is increased with heavier loads, and volume is increased with more exercise or repetitions.

Progressive Resistance Training Checklist

✔ Consult a physician before participating in a progressive resistance exercise program to address any diseases or physical limitations.

✔ Seek guidance from qualified fitness professionals certified through national or international accredited certifying agencies. This is particularly important should the program require modification due to physical limitations or disease.

✔ Maintain neutral body alignment while performing all exercises.

✔ Keep the trunk stable; the shoulder blades are held down and back; the belly is held in tightly toward spine.

✔ Perform approximately eight to twelve, up to fifteen, repetitions of each exercise for all major muscle groups.

✔ Move muscles or muscle groups in a slow, controlled manner, moving through a full range of motion to complete muscle fatigue.

✔ Count two seconds on the lifting (effort) phase and four seconds on the lowering phase of each repetition of an exercise.

✔ Exhale on the effort phase and inhale on the lowering phase of each repetition of an exercise.

✔ Progress gradually; increase the resistance approximately five percent after being able to perform 12 repetitions of an exercise easily.

✔ Perform the necessary static stretches following the program to return muscles to their neutral resting length.

✔ Hold static stretches gently for 15 to 30 seconds.

✔ Pay close attention to areas of chronic tightness. These areas often include the muscles of the calves, front and back of the hip, the back of the thigh (hamstrings), the lower back, the chest, and the front of the shoulder. Perform multiple repetitions for these areas.

Progressive Resistance Training

neutral alignment

muscular endurance

muscular strength

muscular hypertrophy

Basic Exercises: Sample Lower Body Program

Choose one excercise for each muscle group. Perform 8 to 12, up to 15 repetitions, per set.

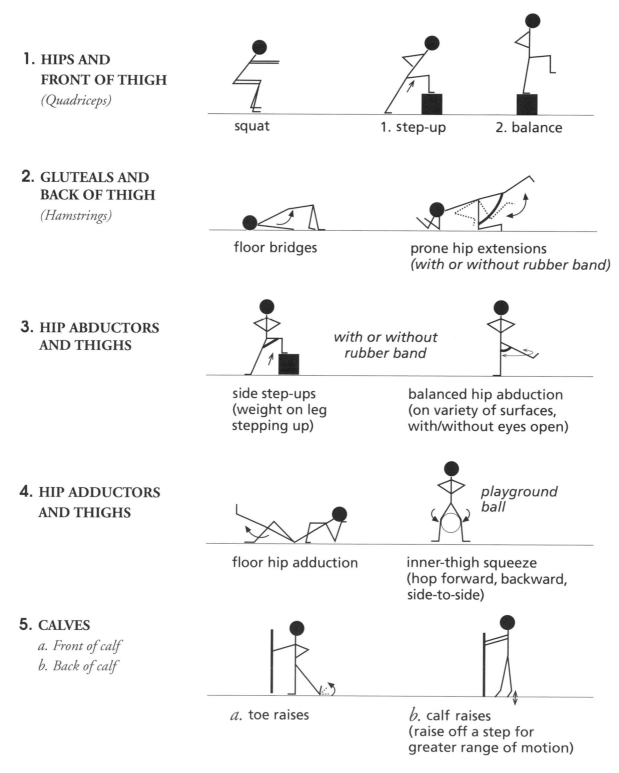

1. HIPS AND FRONT OF THIGH
(Quadriceps)

squat   1. step-up   2. balance

2. GLUTEALS AND BACK OF THIGH
(Hamstrings)

floor bridges   prone hip extensions
(with or without rubber band)

3. HIP ABDUCTORS AND THIGHS

with or without rubber band

side step-ups
(weight on leg
stepping up)

balanced hip abduction
(on variety of surfaces,
with/without eyes open)

4. HIP ADDUCTORS AND THIGHS

playground ball

floor hip adduction

inner-thigh squeeze
(hop forward, backward,
side-to-side)

5. CALVES
a. Front of calf
b. Back of calf

a. toe raises

b. calf raises
(raise off a step for
greater range of motion)

Resistance materials used in the program may include free weights, rubber, cable systems, machines, or simply body weight opposing gravity. Muscles must move resistances or loads that they are not used to moving. They must be overloaded. The program must be changed periodically so that the muscles do not accommodate to the exercises. Muscles that become used to exercises are no longer stimulated to change. Programs must be personalized, based on individual needs. They also must be modified to meet an individual's limitations.

Basic Exercises: *Sample Upper Body/Trunk Program*

Choose one excercise for each muscle group. Perform 8 to 12, up to 15 repetitions, per set.

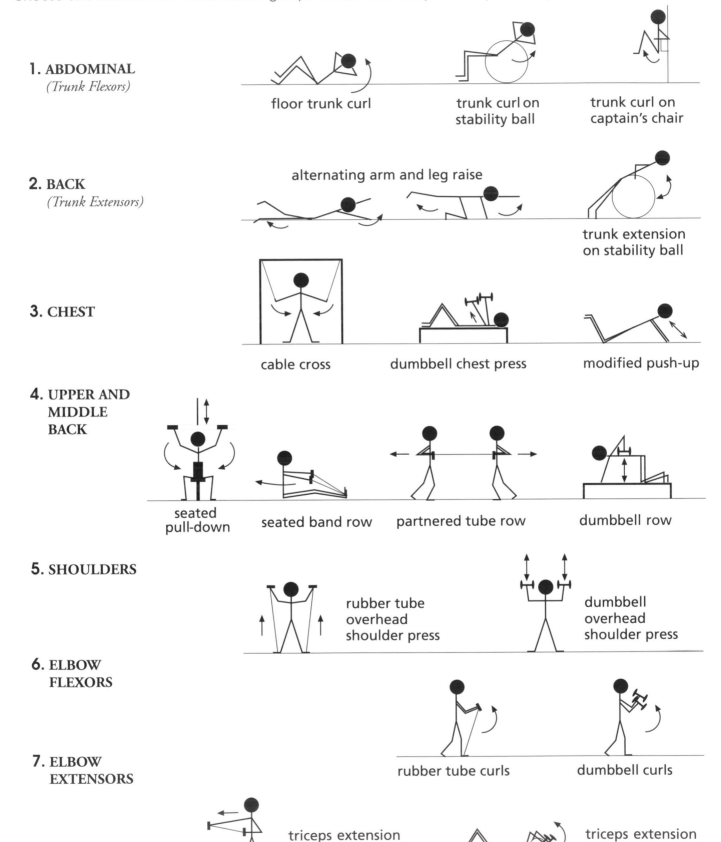

1. ABDOMINAL
(Trunk Flexors)

floor trunk curl

trunk curl on stability ball

trunk curl on captain's chair

2. BACK
(Trunk Extensors)

alternating arm and leg raise

trunk extension on stability ball

3. CHEST

cable cross

dumbbell chest press

modified push-up

4. UPPER AND MIDDLE BACK

seated pull-down

seated band row

partnered tube row

dumbbell row

5. SHOULDERS

rubber tube overhead shoulder press

dumbbell overhead shoulder press

6. ELBOW FLEXORS

rubber tube curls

dumbbell curls

7. ELBOW EXTENSORS

triceps extension with rubber tubing

triceps extension with dumbbell

Phyl and Phyllis's Physiology Phorum

The ACSM and ACE recommendation of a minimum of two sessions per week should include one to three sets of ten to twelve exercises that utilize all of the major muscle groups. The major muscle groups to be included are the chest, upper and lower back, abdominal muscles, the front and back of the arms and legs, and the buttocks. Exercises should be performed in proper neutral body alignment under proper supervision, moving muscles through their full range of motion in a slow, controlled manner. Proper breathing technique should be used; exhaling on the effort phase and inhaling on the lengthening phase of each exercise. Breath holding should be avoided.

In strength training, loads should be sufficient to approach momentary fatique in the muscle or muscle groups while performing eight to twelve repetitions of an exercise. Initially, strength gains are the result of better neurological functioning. Later, strength gains are additionally the result of an increase in the density of muscle fibers. This is called muscular hypertrophy.

To achieve better muscular endurance, more repetitions are performed with less resistance. Muscles exercised for endurance become better equipped to handle tasks of daily living for longer periods of time with less effort. Carrying groceries, briefcases, backpacks, babies, or golf clubs becomes easier.

Strength training stimulates greater muscle protein synthesis as a result of the stress imposed on the existing muscle tissue. The body makes what it needs to handle the work it is going to perform on a regular basis. A day of strength training should be followed by a day of rest for the muscles that were exercised so that they have time and energy to synthesize the additional muscle protein. Protein synthesis in itself utilizes energy. The increase in the muscle mass coupled with the energy cost of building new muscle increases the metabolic rate.

Not only does a progressive resistance program potentially increase the density of muscle, but it can also increase the tissue density in bones, ligaments, and tendons. Strong bones and musculature help to maintain good posture and balance. Strong musculature also helps to keep joints stable and free of injury.

How much of an energy deficit should be created through dietary modification?

How much through exercise?

Phyl and Phyllis's Physiology Phorum

Both severe obesity and excessive thinness place undue stress on healthy vital organ functioning and on the musculosketal system. Both unhealthy body compositions promote disease. This results in diminished quality of life.

Starvation diets, very low-calorie diets, and many fad diets produce fast results on bathroom scales, but do not produce healthy, lasting results. Weight loss resulting from these programs is often the result of a combination of water loss and loss of fat-free mass as opposed to body fat. Loss of fat-free mass means loss of metabolically active tissue and lowered metabolic rate.

Additionally, low calorie often corresponds to low energy. A fatigued individual is not typically enthusiastic about exercise. The desired body weight should be one that is realistic, attainable, and coincides with a healthier body composition. It should also be one that corresponds to frame size. Larger bones and larger musculature weigh more.

Simple Means
to Achieve 1,000 Calories in
Cardiovascular Exercise

- 15- to 20-minute jog or a 20- to 25-minute brisk walk daily

- 20- to 25-minute jog or 30- to 35-minute brisk walk 5 days per week

- 35- to 40-minute jog or 50- to 60-minute brisk walk 3 days per week

It takes an energy deficit of 3,500 calories to lose one pound of fat. If we avoid skipping meals, we can avoid the resulting hunger and overeating. If we also eliminate unconscious snacking and pay attention to portion sizes, it is reasonable to create an energy deficit of 500 calories per day. This would create a 3,500 calorie deficit per week and potentially a one-pound weight loss.

For the sedentary individual, it is also reasonable to begin a cardiovascular exercise program of 1,000 calories per week to add to the energy deficit. The 1,000 calories can be divided into seven, five, or three days, depending on individual time constraints. A daily accumulation of sixty or more minutes (over multiple bouts of cardiovascular exercise if necessary) is frequently recommended to help individuals create a greater calorie deficit. Gradually, the duration and intensity of the cardiovascular exercise should be increased.

For the person who already exercises and uses a particular number of calories per week in cardiovascular exercise, additional calories can be expended by adding new types of exercise or by adjusting the frequency, duration, or intensity of their current activities. An additional 500 to 1,000 calories of exercise can be added if necessary. Barring a medical issue or metabolic disorder, someone who is already exercising regularly is not excessively over-fat. Some individuals may only want to improve their body composition, lose some fat, or become more fit and healthy.

Small increases in exercise and activity add up quickly. For instance, ten extra minutes per exercise session can create at least 500 additional calories per week. Adding extra daily activities such as pacing, using stairs instead of elevators or escalators, and walking to and from restaurants, stores and train stations can also contribute to greater calorie expenditure.

Combined, the energy deficit created from calorie and portion control plus the energy expended in the cardiovascular and other physical activity accumulate to a weight loss of about one to two pounds per week. Though many people desire more rapid results, this is a safe rate of loss in which loss of FFM is minimized and fat will be lost.

Fat is lost when one uses more fat than that which is deposited. We cannot determine or choose areas of fat to be lost. Muscles do not use the fat that surrounds them. Fat is released from storage when epinephrine stimulates an enzyme in fat tissue. This stimulation along with other factors causes fat to be released into the blood and become available to cells to fuel their work.

Some people carry more fat in their abdominal areas, some in their hips and thighs. For better or worse, our heredity and many other factors dictate where we deposit fat. The same is true for where we release fat.

Cardiovascular exercise causes the adrenal gland to produce epinephrine, resulting in the release of fat from fat storage. When aerobically-trained muscle cells perform activities, their more numerous mitochondria allow for greater oxygen utilization. The greater the use of oxygen, the more released fat is used.

A good weight-management program is one that combines moderate caloric reduction with a sound nutritional program. Combining a healthy, balanced diet with a regular exercise program and a general increase in activity level is a healthy way to manage weight. The emphasis should be on achieving a healthy body composition while maintaining one's metabolic rate.

The exercise program should include both cardiovascular exercise and progressive resistance training. Moderately challenging cardiovascular exercise will help gradually use fat storage. Progressive resistance training helps to maintain muscle mass, bone density, and therefore metabolic rate.

Weight goals should be realistic, attainable, and consistent with one's age and heredity. They also should be reached over a reasonable period of time. Quick weight loss is tempting but is not typically associated with healthy methods. Active pursuit of goals through good habits over the long term will achieve a body composition that reflects healthier physiology.

Good Weight-Management Program

1 use fat through increased activity + ...

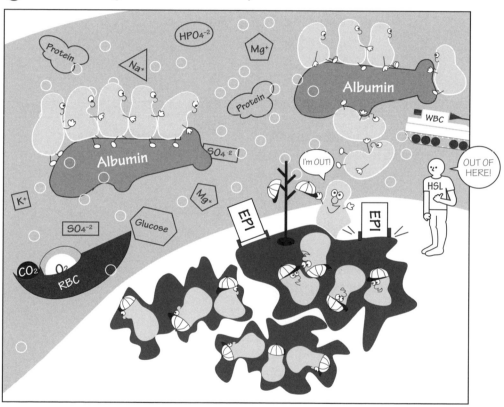

2 maintain muscle mass + ...

Good Weight-Management Program

3 avoid consuming excess calories + . . .

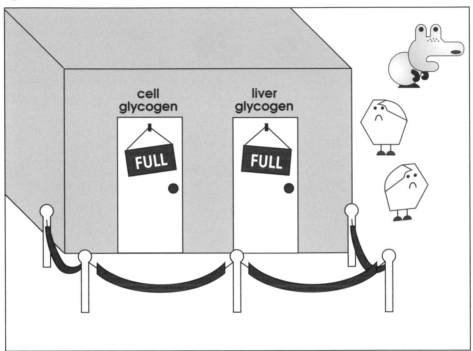

4 results in making less fat + . . .

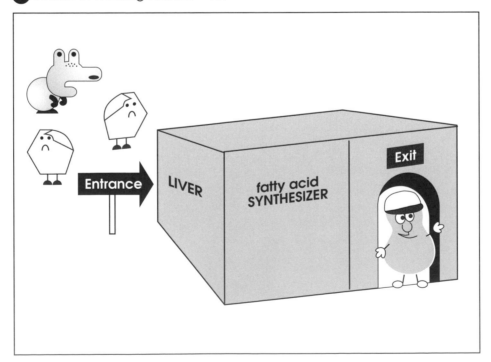

Good Weight-Management Program

5 less fat deposited + . . .

= body composition improvement

Essential Nutrients

Chapter 8
Vitamins

Vitamins:
Enzyme Activators

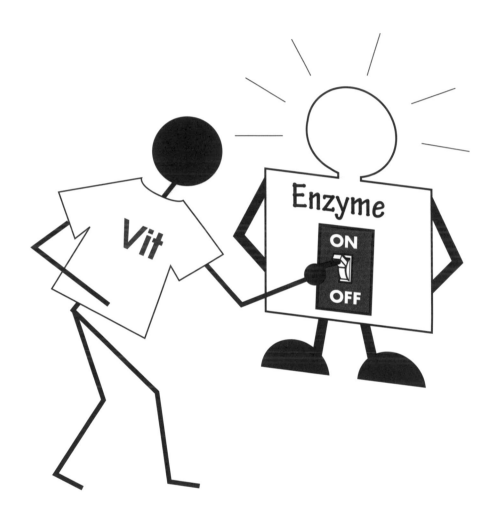

Carbohydrates, fats, and proteins are essential nutrients that are both energy-yielding and necessary for the repair, maintenance, and construction of body tissue. They are derived from both plant and animal sources.

Vitamins are also essential nutrients that occur naturally in both plant and animal food sources. Vitamins may also be called micronutrients because they are required in very small amounts.

Vitamins function as important assistants, or coenzymes in numerous body functions. Enzymes are the activators or catalysts in the chemical reactions that take place throughout the body. Without coenzymes, enzymes do not work.

Vitamins:
Water-Soluble and Fat-Soluble

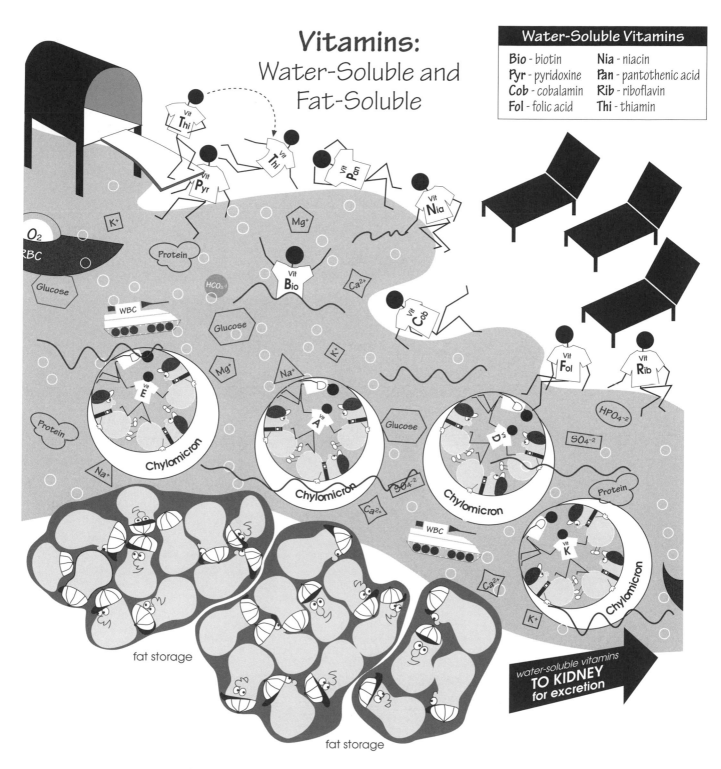

Vitamins are designated as either water-soluble or fat-soluble. The water-soluble vitamins are the B vitamins and vitamin C. The fat-soluble vitamins are vitamins A, D, E, and K.

The B vitamins are thiamin, riboflavin, niacin, pyridoxine, folate, cobalamin, biotin, and pantothenic acid. The designation of solubility indicates the manner in which a vitamin enters the body and is transported, stored, and excreted. Water-soluble vitamins enter the blood directly from the small intestine and are carried freely in the blood plasma. They are used immediately. Excess water-soluble vitamins are excreted at the kidney.

145

The Water-Soluble Vitamins
B Vitamins in Energy Production

The water-soluble vitamins do not yield energy, but several of them do participate in energy production or the making of ATP.

Water-Soluble Vitamins:
Jobs in the Body

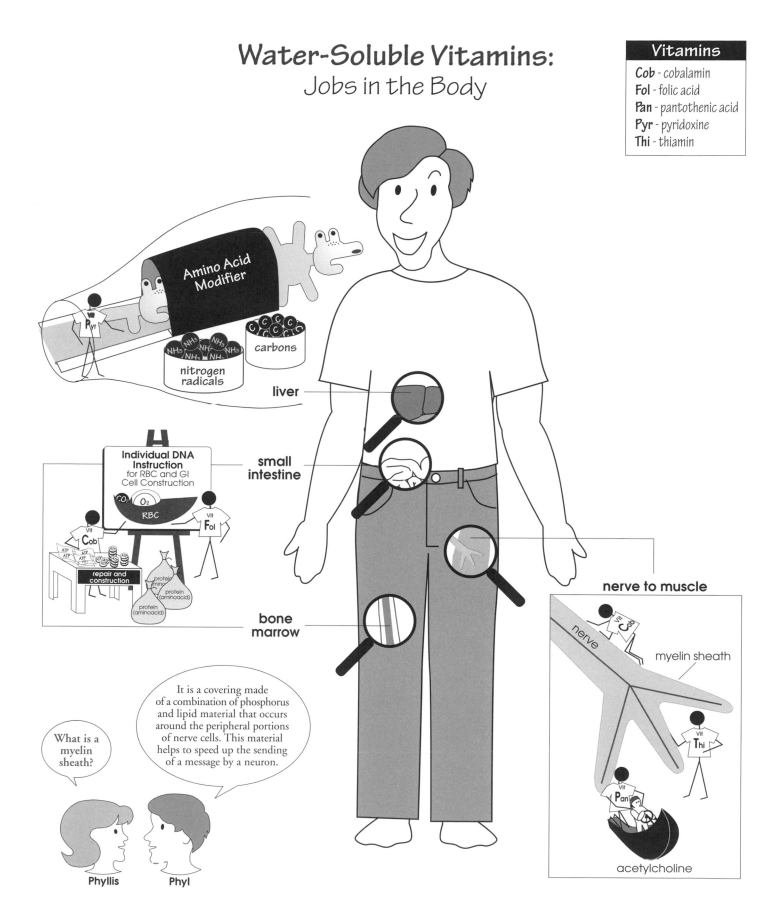

Some vitamins are involved in the building and repair of cells, particularly gastrointestinal and red blood cells. Other water-soluble vitamins are involved in the protection of the nervous system.

Water-Soluble Vitamins: Vitamin C
Jobs in Our Bodies

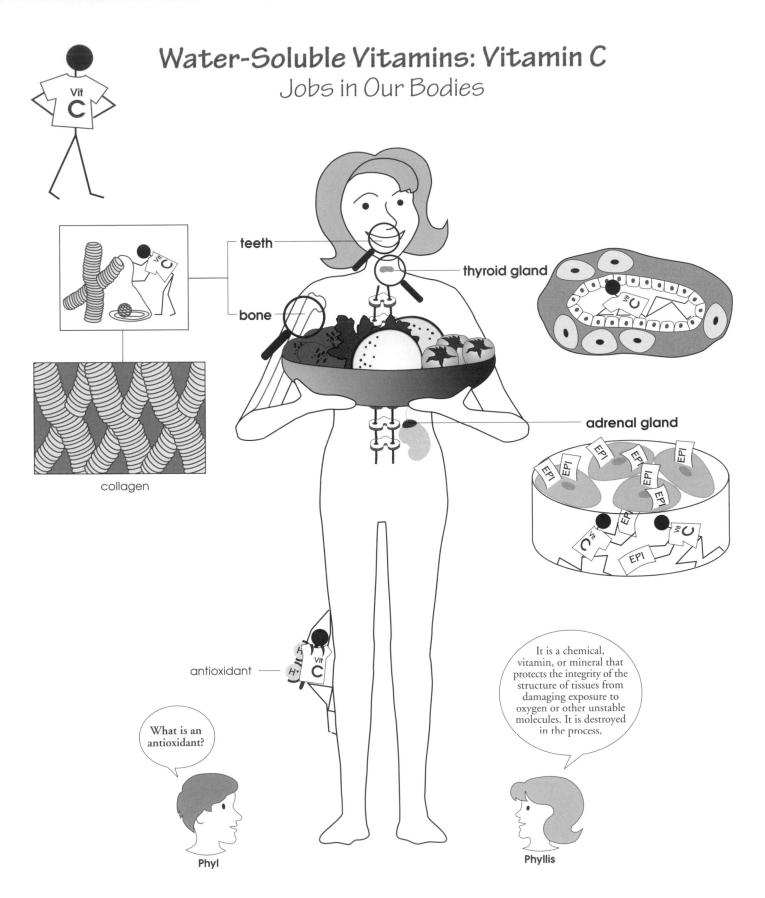

collagen

teeth

thyroid gland

bone

adrenal gland

antioxidant

What is an antioxidant?

Phyl

It is a chemical, vitamin, or mineral that protects the integrity of the structure of tissues from damaging exposure to oxygen or other unstable molecules. It is destroyed in the process.

Phyllis

Vitamin C is important in making the protein collagen. Collagen provides the strong infrastructure for bones and teeth, in addition to several other body tissues. Vitamin C is also involved in making such hormones as thyroid hormone and epinephrine. Potatoes, spinach, peppers, and tomatoes are some good sources of vitamin C.

Water-Soluble Vitamins:
Food Sources

Water-Soluble Vitamins

Bio - biotin	**Nia** - niacin
Pyr - pyridoxine	**Pan** - pantothenic acid
Cob - cobalamin	**Rib** - riboflavin
Fol - folic acid	**Thi** - thiamin

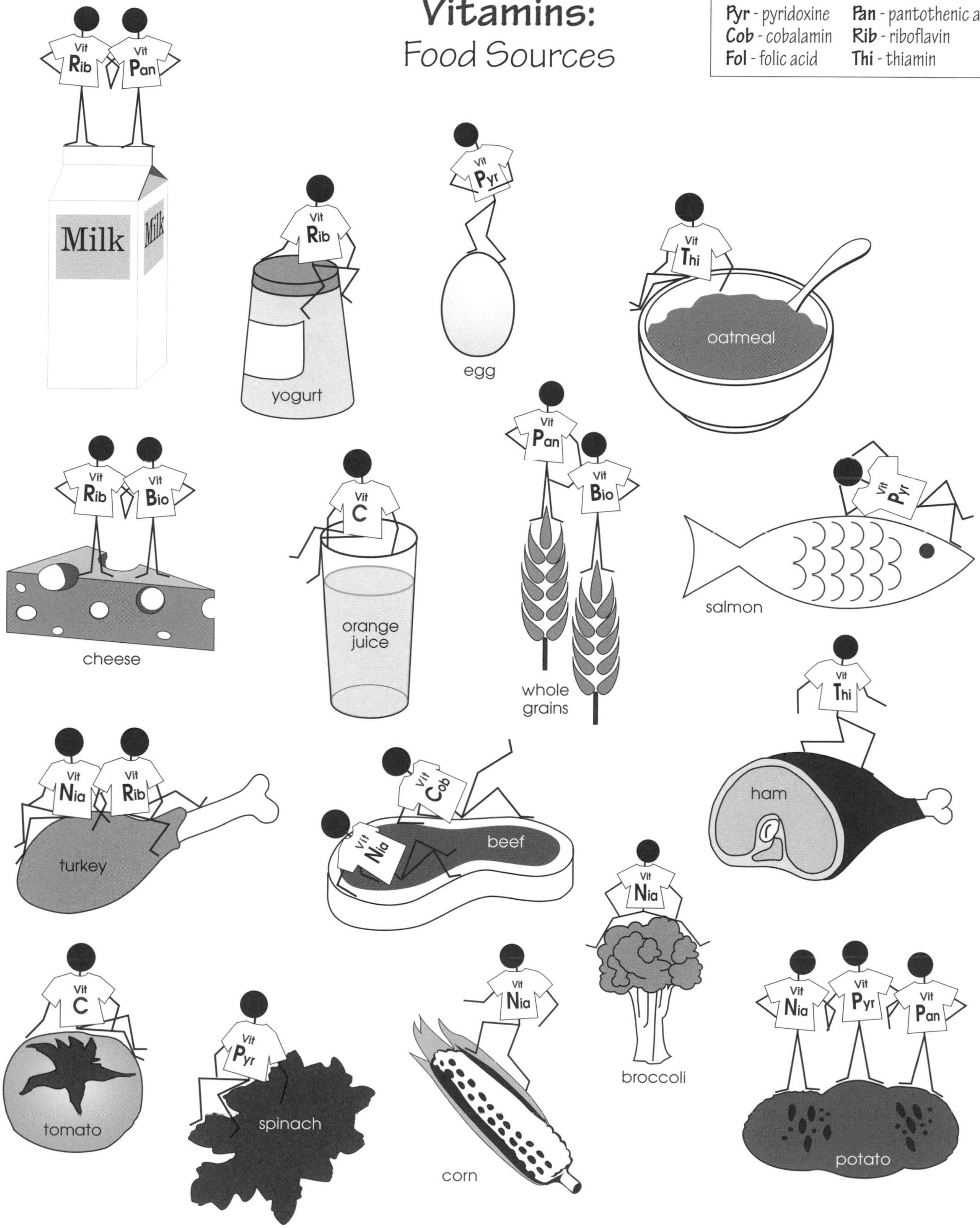

Vit Rib Vit Pan — Milk

Vit Rib — yogurt

Vit Pyr — egg

Vit Thi — oatmeal

Vit Rib Vit Bio — cheese

Vit C — orange juice

Vit Pan Vit Bio — whole grains

Vit Pyr — salmon

Vit Nia Vit Rib — turkey

Vit Cob Vit Nia — beef

Vit Thi — ham

Vit Nia — broccoli

Vit C — tomato

Vit Pyr — spinach

Vit Nia — corn

Vit Nia Vit Pyr Vit Pan — potato

There are many food sources containing the B vitamins. These are a few examples.

How Fat-Soluble Vitamins
Enter the Body

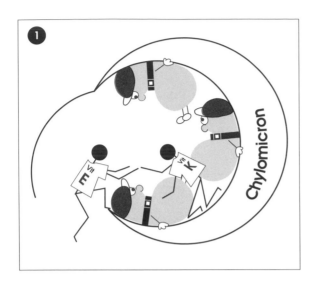

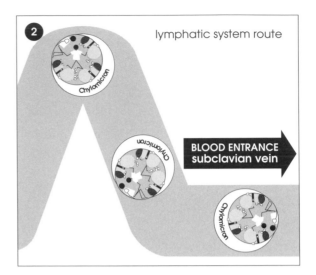

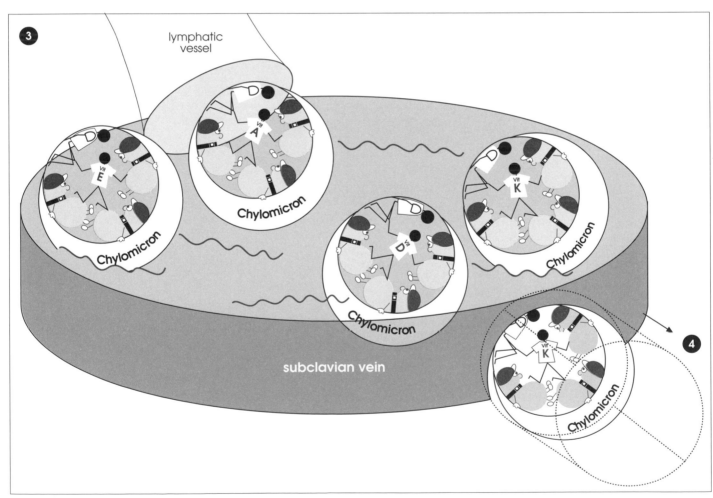

Fat-soluble vitamins enter the blood via the same route as fats. They travel in chylomicrons.
Fat-soluble vitamins are stored in fat tissue or in the liver, and are not readily excreted.
The stored vitamins can be used over a period of time.

How Fat-Soluble Vitamins Enter the Body

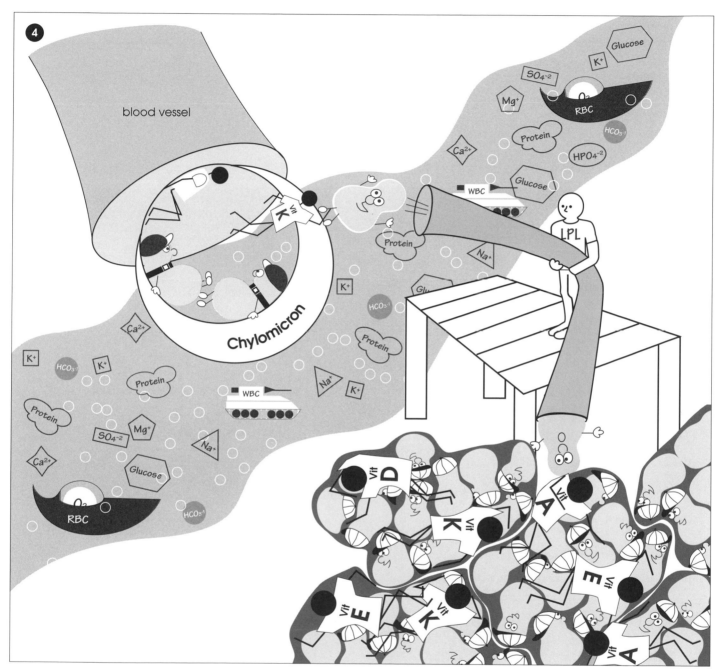

triglyceride storage

Fat-Soluble Vitamins:
Vitamin A

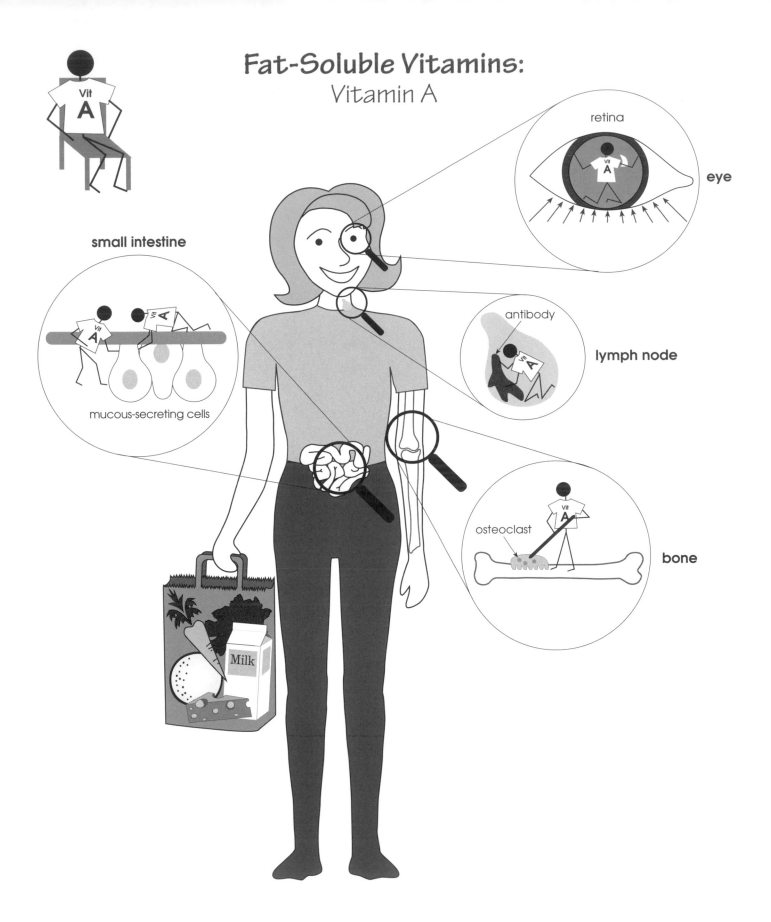

small intestine

mucous-secreting cells

retina

eye

antibody

lymph node

osteoclast

bone

Milk

Vitamin A has many jobs in our bodies, including the maintenance of night vision, a strong immune system, strong bones, and healthy gastrointestinal cells. Vitamin A is found in carrots, cantaloupe, spinach, milk, and cheese, among other sources.

Fat-Soluble Vitamins:
Vitamin D

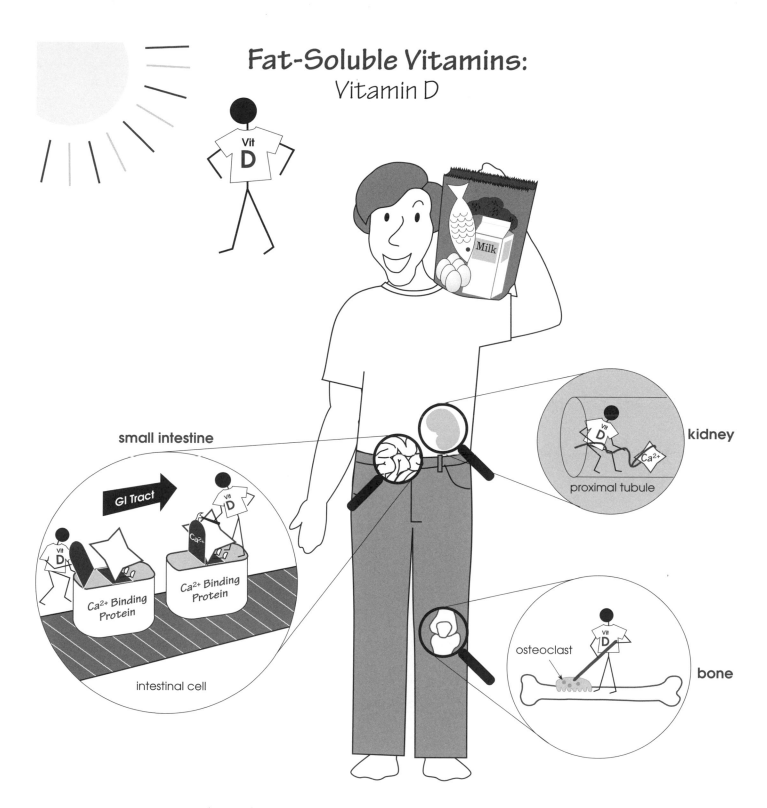

Vitamin D can be made in the body in a very complex manner, provided that our skin is exposed to adequate sunlight. Some food sources also contain added vitamin D. They are said to be fortified with vitamin D.

Vitamin D's work in the body is primarily involved in the maintenance of strong bones. Through various mechanisms, vitamin D ensures that the body has enough of the mineral calcium to build strong bones. Vitamin D ensures absorption of calcium by helping to make the protein carrier that brings calcium into the intestinal cells. It also prevents the loss of calcium at the kidney. Calcium is essential for many other body functions.

Fat-Soluble Vitamins:
E and K

Vitamin E is an antioxidant. It protects our body's tissues, particularly lung tissues, from being destroyed. In this protective role, vitamin E is itself destroyed instead of the tissue structure.

Vitamin K, like vitamin D, can be made in the body. Vitamin K is made in the small intestine. This vitamin is involved in the making of several proteins necessary for blood clotting. Clotting uses materials made by vitamin K to quickly stop bleeding after we cut ourselves.

Fat-Soluble Vitamins:
E and K

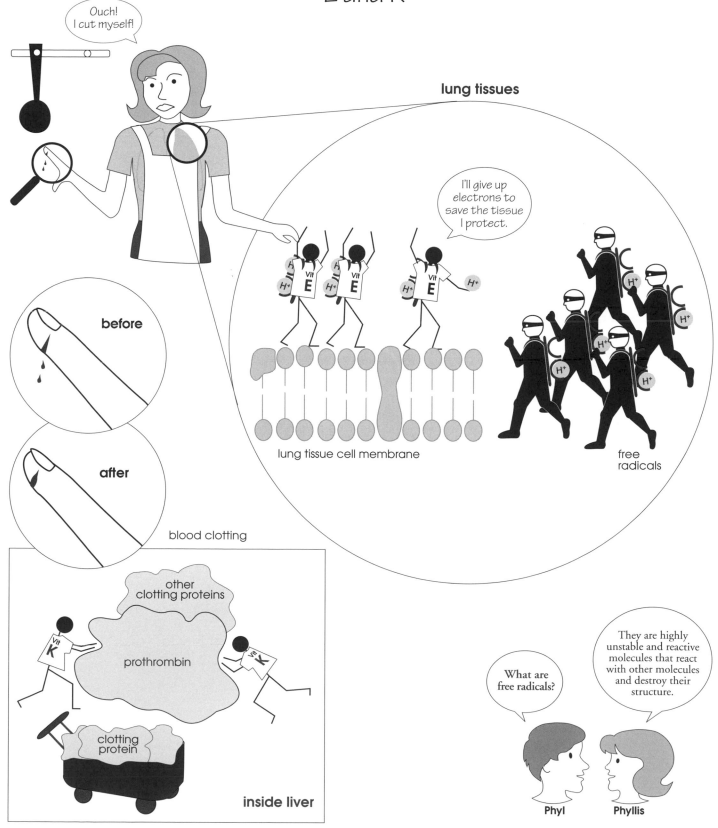

Essential Nutrients

Chapter 9
Water

Body Fluid:
A Soup

Though we do not often think of it as a nutrient, water is as essential a nutrient as carbohydrates, fats, proteins, and vitamins. The adult human body is made of 55 percent to 65 percent water, or fluid. The body fluid is not void of matter, but is much like a soup, comprised of such dissolved ingredients as vitamins, minerals, glucose, amino acids, proteins, blood cells, and gases.

Intracellular Fluid

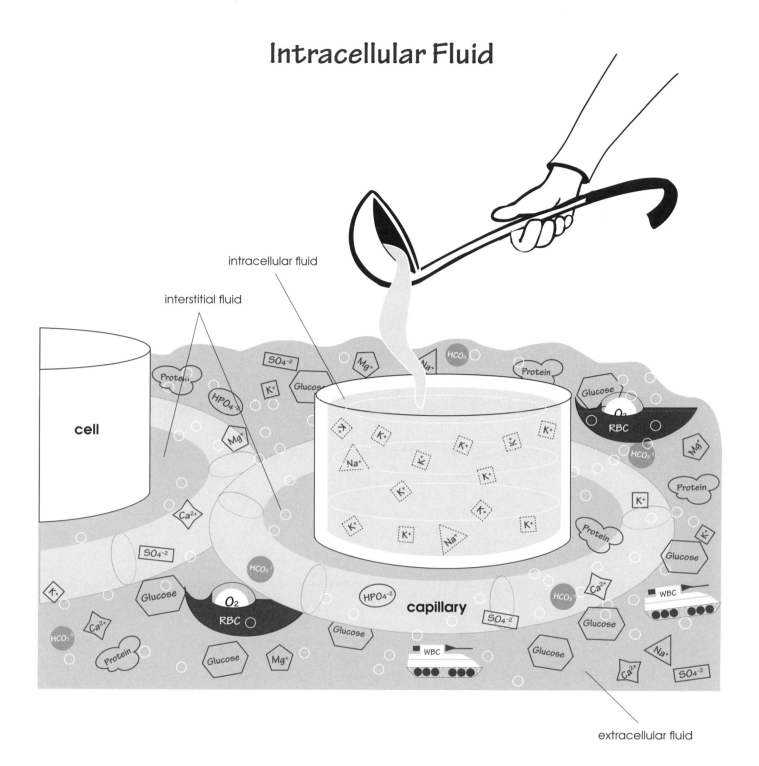

The body is divided into intracellular and extracellular fluid compartments. The composition of the "soup" is different in each of the body's compartments. The intracellular fluid is the fluid inside of the cells. The composition of the intracellular fluid is specific to the inside of cells and differs from that outside of the cell.

The composition of minerals dissolved in our body fluids is important. Some minerals—particularly potassium—may be more abundant in the intracellular fluid; some—particularly sodium—are more abundant in the extracellular fluid. The composition of dissolved minerals in body fluid, both inside and outside of cells is related to body functions.

Extracellular Fluid

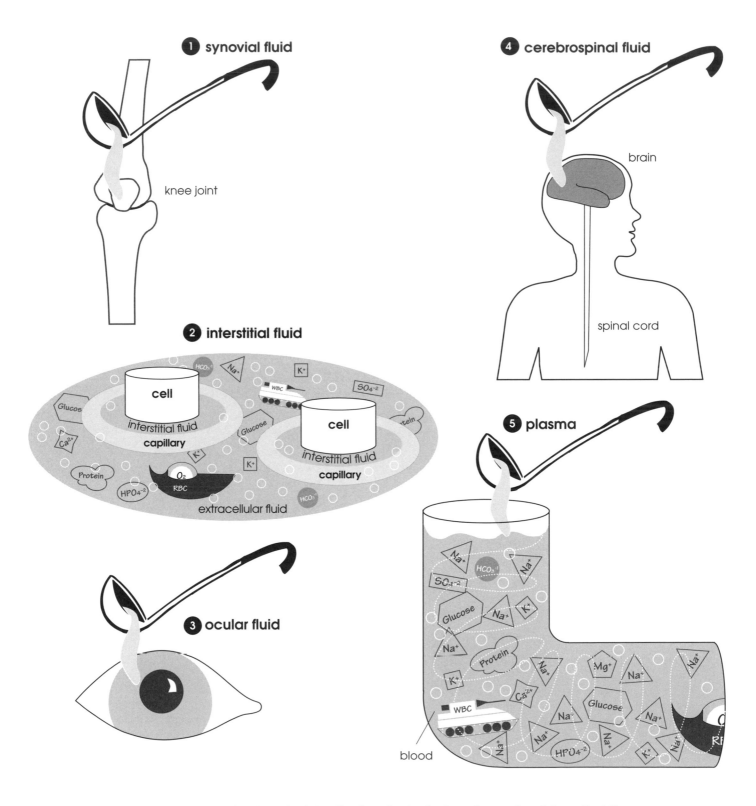

1 synovial fluid

knee joint

2 interstitial fluid

cell

interstitial fluid

capillary

cell

interstitial fluid

capillary

extracellular fluid

Glucose

HCO_3^{-1}

Na^+

WBC

K^+

SO_4^{-2}

Ca^{2+}

K^+

O_2

RBC

Protein

HPO_4^{-2}

K^+

HCO_3

Protein

Glucose

3 ocular fluid

4 cerebrospinal fluid

brain

spinal cord

5 plasma

Na^+

HCO_3^{-1}

Na^+

SO_4^{-2}

Glucose

Na^+

K^+

Na^+

Protein

Na^+

Mg^+

Na^+

K^+

Ca^{2+}

Glucose

Na^+

WBC

Na^+

Na^+

Na^+

HPO_4^{-2}

K^+

Na^+

blood

The extracellular fluid is all of the fluid in the body found outside of the cells. This fluid includes the fluid of the blood, called plasma, the interstitial fluid, which is found between cells, and the cerebrospinal fluid, which nourishes and protects the brain and spinal cord. The extracellular fluid also includes protective fluids such as the ocular fluid of the eye and the synovial fluid of some joints.

Perspiration

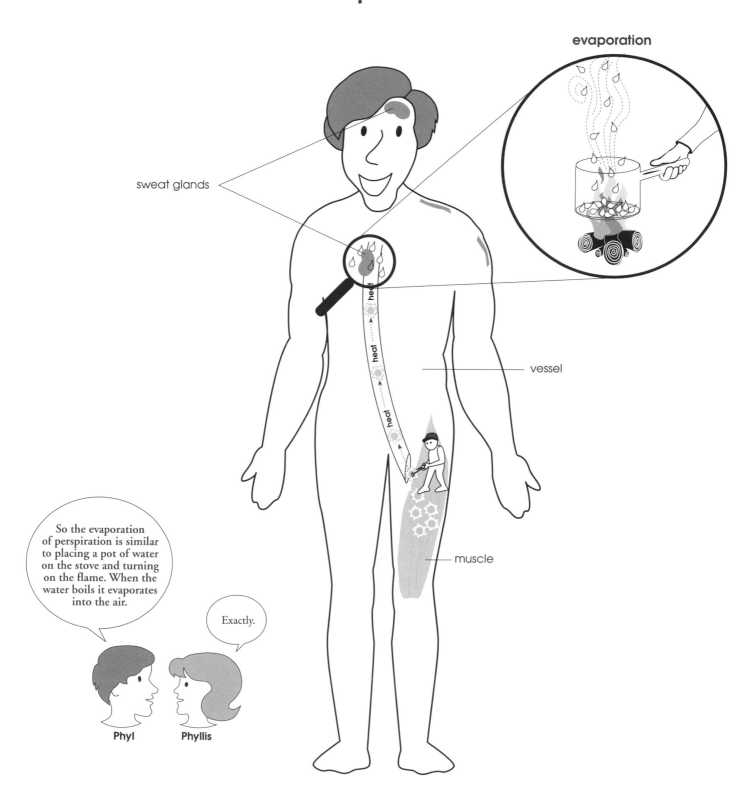

evaporation

sweat glands

vessel

muscle

So the evaporation of perspiration is similar to placing a pot of water on the stove and turning on the flame. When the water boils it evaporates into the air.

Exactly.

Phyl   **Phyllis**

Water is an essential participant in the proper functioning of the human body. For example, it is involved in temperature regulation. The heat produced by muscles during exercise is carried in the blood plasma to the blood vessels at the skin surface. Sweat glands produce perspiration on the skin surface. Then the heat in the blood vessels causes the perspiration to evaporate. This process cools the body.

Blood Pressure

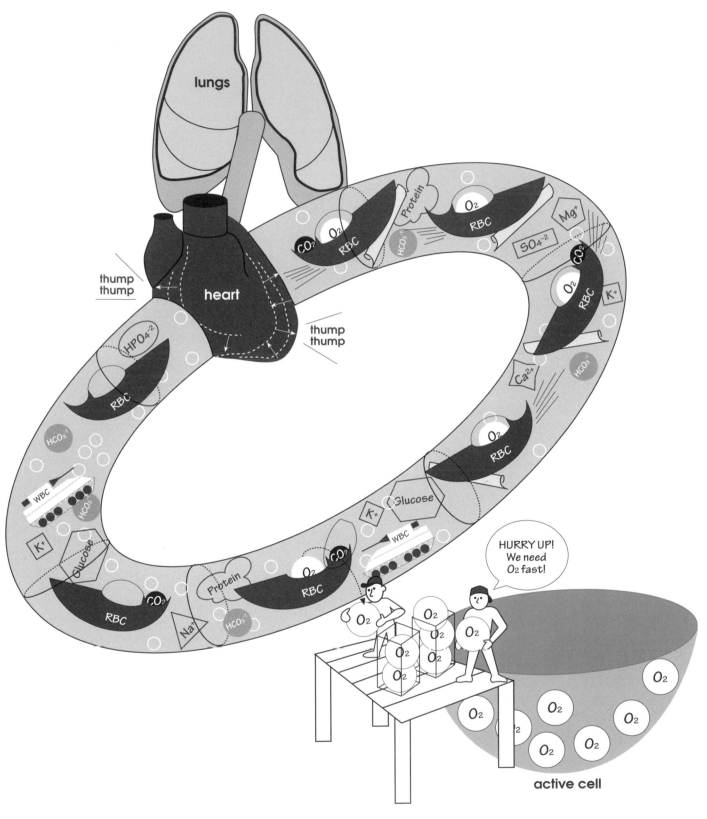

Water is a major component of plasma, which fills our blood vessels and helps to create our blood pressure. Adequate blood pressure is essential for speedy transportation of nutrients to cells and waste products from cells. This is necessary both when the body is exercising and when it is at rest.

Thirst

Water is involved in temperature regulation, maintenance of blood pressure, transportation of materials to and from cells and all chemical reactions in the body. Fluid protects the brain and spinal cord, as well as the joints and eyes. It is as essential a nutrient as the energy-yielding nutrients and vitamins. The fluid volume throughout the body is carefully regulated. The volume of blood plasma is continually monitored. Low volume is detected by various mechanisms that ultimately stimulate thirst and cause us to drink and replenish our fluids. Much water may be lost during exercise due to perspiration. It must be replenished.

Maintenance of fluid balance means having the appropriate volume of fluid in each of the body's fluid compartments. Various receptors throughout the body monitor the constitution of the blood plasma.

Osmoreceptors are located in the brain. As blood flows through the brain, the osmoreceptors measure the concentration of dissolved substances in the blood. This can be described as the thickness of the "soup."

The baroreceptors in large blood vessels respond to blood pressure levels that either exceed or go below that which is necessary to maintain normal blood pressure. The vessels must be filled in order to maintain blood pressure.

Special kidney cells measure the blood pressure in the kidney blood vessels. If pressure is high or low, fluid is either immediately lost in the urine, or retained in the body.

Water loss or retention at the kidney is achieved through various mechanisms. Among these is the retention or loss of the mineral sodium in the kidney tubules.

In the body, fluid tends to move to places where the most dissolved particles occur. Reabsorbing sodium from the kidney tubule causes water to stay in the blood plasma, rather than be excreted in the urine.

Two hormones regulate sodium and water retention at the kidney. One is aldosterone, which is produced by the adrenal gland. The other is antidiuretic hormone (ADH), which is produced by the pituitary gland in the brain. These hormones are secreted in response to low blood pressure or highly concentrated blood plasma, respectively. Together they cause retention of both sodium and water at the kidney and stimulate thirst. Fluid balance is therefore restored.

Thirst

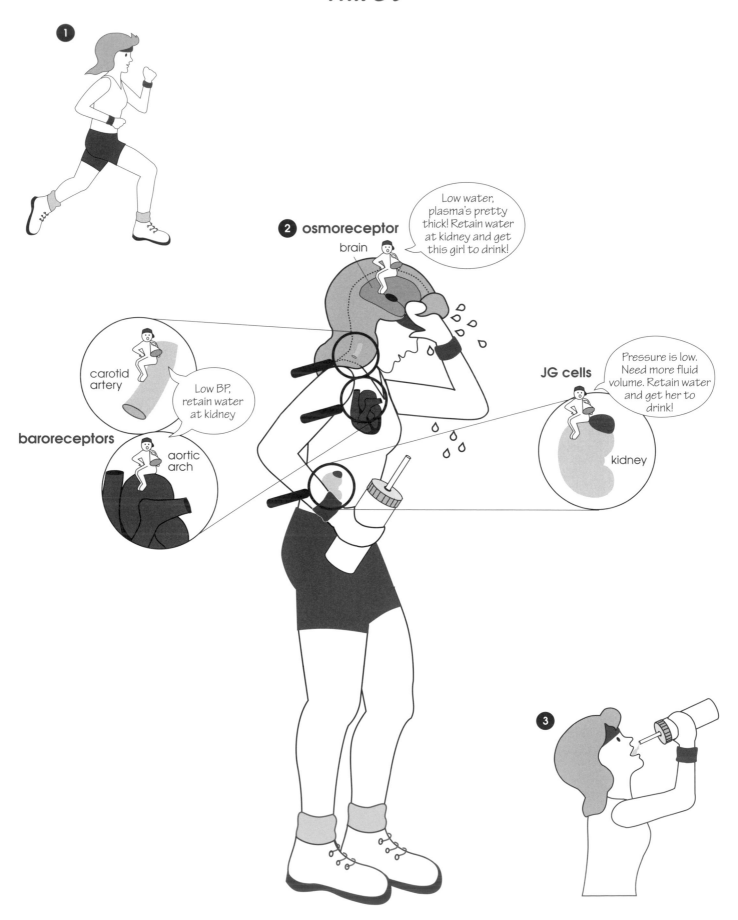

What is blood pressure?
How is it measured?
What is hypertension?

Phyl and Phyllis's Physiology Phorum

The cardiovascular system consists of the heart muscle and the blood vessels, the arteries and veins. The heart is a strong muscular pump that pumps blood to the lungs for gas exchange. It also pumps oxygen-rich blood throughout the body.

Blood is pumped out to tissues through a closed piping system of arteries of varying size. It is then returned from tissues by way of a piping system of veins of varying size.

This system of blood vessels is not rigid, but pliable. It varies throughout in its pliability. The system must be able to accommodate the rhythmic pulsations of the heart as well as fluctuations in pressure.

Blood is delivered selectively. Arterioles leading to capillaries rhythmically open and close depending on the second-to-second nutrient and oxygen demands of tissues. Speed and force of delivery must be appropriate.

Sometimes blood flows more slowly and less forcefully. Sometimes blood and its constituents surge through blood vessels like a rushing river. It flows turbulently and at high speeds to active tissues. Arterioles leading to active tissues open and those leading to inactive tissues contract or narrow.

Blood pressure is the force exerted by this rushing river of blood and its constituents on the inner walls of arteries. Blood pressure pushes blood and its nutrients and oxygen from larger blood vessels to the tiniest of capillaries that serve tissue cells.

Blood pressure is measured by an instrument called a sphygmomanometer. Two measurements of blood pressure are taken: systolic and diastolic. Systolic blood pressure is the force of blood exerted on the inner wall of arteries when the heart is contracted or in systole. Diastolic blood pressure is the force exerted when the heart is relaxed or in diastole.

Systolic pressure occurs when the heart is pumping a load of blood into an already-filled piping system of blood vessels. This creates higher pressure than when the heart is at rest or filling with blood during diastole. Normal blood pressures range from 90/60 to about 120/80. Blood pressure fluctuates according to body position and activity level.

The inner walls of arteries consist of a layer of cells that smoothly connect together, protecting the tissue beneath them. This protective layer is called the endothelial lining. It is designed to withstand the second-to-second fluctuations in pressure exerted against it.

Blood pressure is created by a combination of factors. The first factor is the push of the heart muscle as it pumps blood into the closed piping system. The second factor is the tightness of the piping system. The volume of fluid that fills the piping system influences its tightness. The tightness is also a matter of how many arterioles are open and how many are closed. If more are closed, the system is tighter and pressures are greater. If more are open, such as when the large muscles of the body are performing cardiovascular activity, pressures are lower.

The pressure resulting from constricted arterioles is called peripheral resistance; the greater the number of constricted arterioles, the greater the peripheral resistance. The heart has to exert more pressure to overcome this resistance.

Blood must arrive at active tissues quickly enough to deliver sufficient oxygen and nutrients. However, speed and pressure must be appropriate. When blood is not immediately required, turbulence and high pressure are not only unnecessary, but may in fact damage the smooth cell-to-cell connections of the endothelial lining. Chronically elevated blood pressure is a disorder called hypertension. A resting blood pressure of more than 120/80 is considered pre-hypertensive. A blood pressure of 140/90, once considered mildly hypertensive, is now considered high blood pressure and demands medical attention.

Hypertension damages the endothelial lining and exposes vulnerable tissues not only to more damage by elevated blood pressure, but also to invasion of this tissue by other blood constituents. The result of this damage and invasion contributes to the development of atherosclerosis. Atherosclerosis and hypertension are two of the most common diseases of the cardiovascular system.

Blood Pressure

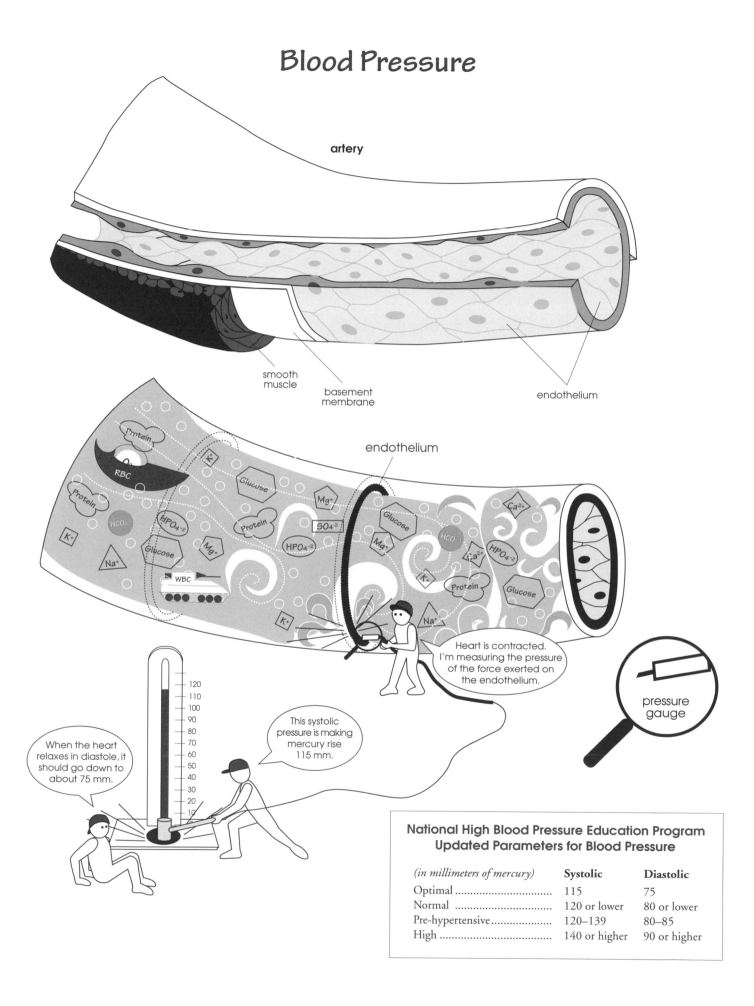

How do diet and exercise help treat and prevent hypertension over the long term?

Regular cardiovascular exercise and a moderate-calorie, nutrient-dense, low-fat, low-sodium diet are beneficial to a hypertensive person for several reasons. First of all, excess body fat is lost so that the heart does not struggle to pump blood through a disproportionately over-fat body.

Phyl and Phyllis's Physiology Phorum

A heart that is exercised on a regular basis is a stronger and more efficient pump. The push of the heart muscle into the closed piping system requires less effort. More blood is pumped with greater ease and fewer beats. A diet low in sodium prevents excess fluid retention in the piping system.

Regular cardiovascular exercise helps to relax the arteries and stimulate the growth of additional networks of blood vessels. This loosening or spreading out of the piping system creates less peripheral resistance. These factors interact to result in lowered blood pressure at rest and during activity.

If hypertension cannot be controlled through diet and exercise, several antihypertensive medications may be prescribed. Once blood pressure is controlled, progressive resistance is encouraged. With a physician's approval, a low to moderate resistance program may be added to cardiovascular exercise.

Essential Nutrients

Chapter 10
Minerals

Minerals:
Ions

As previously discussed, the composition of the "soup" in each of the body's fluid compartments is different. The dissolved minerals specific to that compartment make each one different.

Minerals are small inorganic atoms. Many of these atoms are metals. Some examples of minerals that are metals are sodium, potassium, calcium, magnesium, iron, and copper. Some minerals such as chloride and phosphorus are nonmetals.

All atoms possess subatomic particles. These are equal numbers of protons, neutrons and electrons. Protons are positively charged particles; electrons are negatively charged particles; neutrons are electrically neutral. Therefore all atoms are electrically neutral.

Atoms that are metals tend to lose one or more of their electrons. These metals therefore carry positive electrical charges. Those that are not metals may gain extra electrons. These, therefore, may carry negative electrical charges. Electrically charged substances that occur in the human body are called electrolytes or ions.

Those ions that are positively charged are called cations and those that are negatively charged, anions. Ions move back and forth, to and from the fluid compartments of the body. This movement is responsible for many bodily functions including nerve transmission and muscular contraction.

170

Minerals:
Cations and Anions in the Body

Sodium is the most prevalent extracellular cation. It is involved in nerve transmission and muscular contraction. Sodium is also particularly important in maintenance of fluid balance.

Chloride is a predominant extracellular anion, but moves between fluid compartments. Chloride combines with hydrogen in the stomach to make hydrochloric acid during the digestive process. The chloride anion follows the sodium cation at the kidney, so when sodium is retained for purposes of fluid balance, chloride follows.

Potassium is a predominant intracellular cation. It is particularly important in nerve transmission and in the contraction of all muscle tissue throughout the human body.

Calcium is an extracellular cation. It is involved in so many important functions that blood levels of calcium are closely regulated within the body. Calcium is also found combined with phosphate to make the crystals in bone and teeth.

Phosphate is an intracellular anion. It is found in bones and teeth as part of ATP, cell membranes, and the genetic instruction materials DNA and RNA.

Magnesium is an intracellular cation. It is involved in nerve transmission, muscular contraction and relaxation as well as carbohydrate metabolism. It is also part of DNA and RNA.

Minerals have many jobs in the body that are vital to life. Like vitamins and water, they are essential nutrients.

Major Minerals

The major minerals are sodium, chloride, potassium, calcium, phosphorus (occurring as the phosphate ion), and magnesium. These minerals can be found in a wide variety of foods.

Major Minerals:
Nerve Transmission and Muscular Contraction

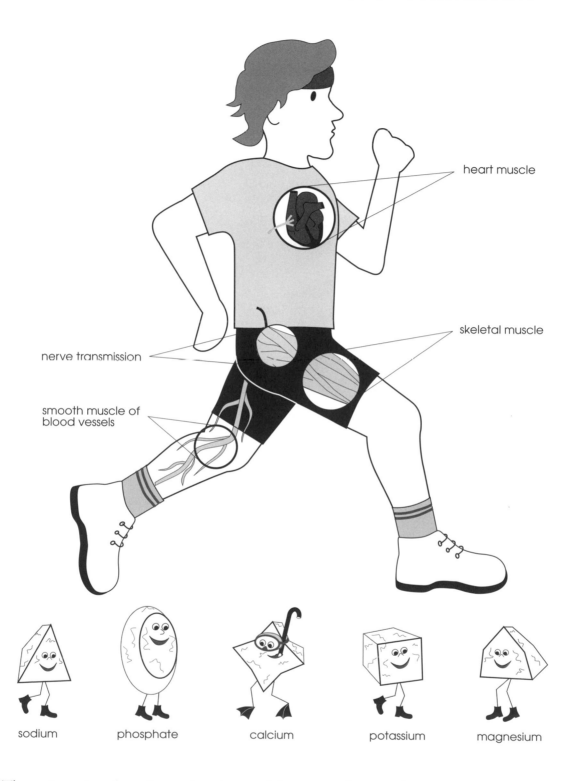

The major minerals sodium, phosphate, calcium, potassium, and magnesium are involved in nerve transmission and contraction of muscle tissue throughout the body. Sodium, potassium, calcium, and magnesium ions are important in nerve transmission. Calcium, sodium, potassium, and magnesium ions are essential for the contraction and relaxation of muscle tissue throughout the body. Phosphate is part of the ATP that fuels the contraction.

Calcium:
Teeth and Bones

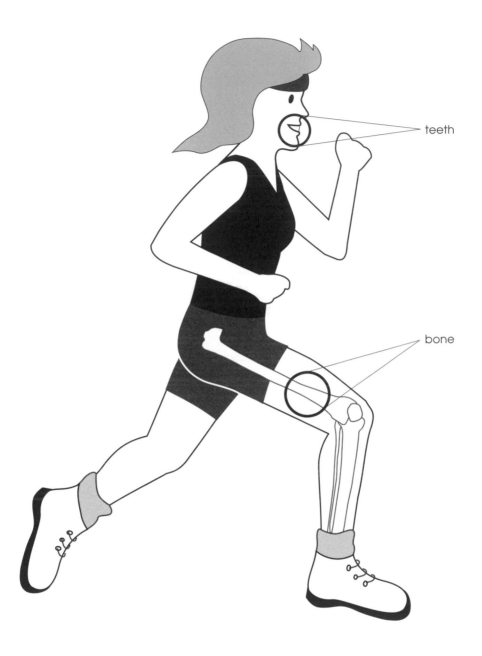

Though calcium is used throughout the body for numerous functions, it is most familiar as that which combines with phosphorus to form the crystals in bones and teeth. These crystals are called hydroxyapatite crystals.

The densely packed crystals in teeth allow them to withstand the continuous compressive forces of biting and chewing. The human skeleton provides a strong framework to which our muscles are attached. It also serves a second function—that of a calcium reservoir.

Mobilization of Calcium from Bone

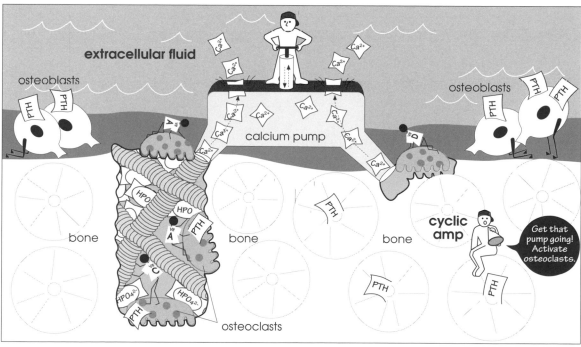

Calcium is such an important mineral in the body that its blood levels are continually monitored by specialized cells of the parathyroid glands. When blood-calcium drops below a desirable level, parathyroid hormone is secreted into the blood. Parathyroid hormone activates special calcium pumps that occur in bone tissue. It also activates bone-dissolving (resorbing) cells called osteoclasts. When this resorption process is activated, calcium from bone is removed and sent out into the blood for use in nerve transmission, muscular contraction, blood clotting and numerous other functions.

If calcium blood levels are elevated, calcium is removed from the blood and deposited into the bone or excreted at the kidney. A thyroid hormone called calcitonin influences this process. The calcium exchange takes place continuously. Therefore it is imperative that bones are strong and dense, and stocked with plenty of calcium.

What is bone resorption?

Phyllis

It is the process of bone removal or dissolving old bone materials.

Phyl

Bone Building and Remodeling

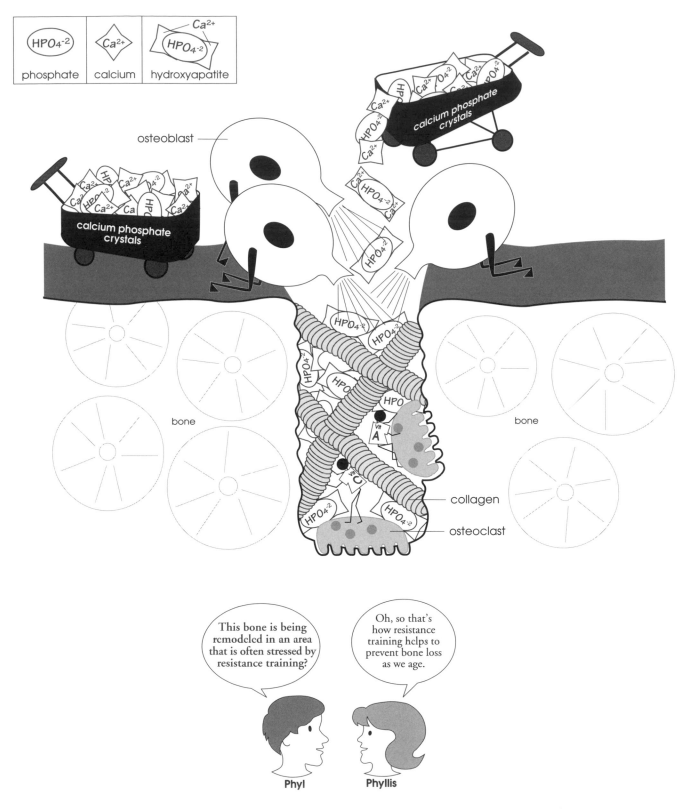

Consistent weight-bearing and resistance exercise stresses bone, thereby stimulating the building of strong, dense, bones during the growth years and throughout life. A calcium-rich diet is equally important. Milk products provide the best source of calcium because they contain ingredients conducive to the absorption of calcium.

Trace Minerals

The trace minerals are iron, zinc, iodine, selenium, copper, manganese, fluoride, chromium, and molybdenum. While trace minerals are not as abundant in the body as the major minerals, they are equally important.

Trace Minerals:
Iron

They are as essential to health as are the major minerals. Iron is so important in the body that the intestinal cells that absorb it are specially equipped with proteins to either transfer it to a carrier in the blood or store it for future use.

Special proteins in the blood carry iron to bone marrow and other cells. Blood cells of all types are made in the bone marrow. Red blood cells contain a protein that carries oxygen. This protein is called hemoglobin, of which iron is a major component. Iron also occurs in muscle as part of an oxygen-binding protein called myoglobin. Iron plays a crucial role in the final biochemical processes of the production of ATP. Iron is also involved in the manufacture of important materials in the body such as collagen, neurotransmitters, and hormones. Iron is a precious mineral. It is brought in, stored, and continually recycled in the body.

Exercise requires plenty of healthy red blood cells to deliver oxygen, and sufficient ATP to fuel the work. A diet that provides adequate iron is essential. Meat, fish, poultry, and spinach are good sources of iron. Vitamin C helps the body absorb iron.

Trace Minerals:
Iron

Minerals
Cu - copper
Cr - chromium
Fl - fluoride
I - iodine
Fe - iron
Mn - manganese
Se - selenium
Zn - zinc

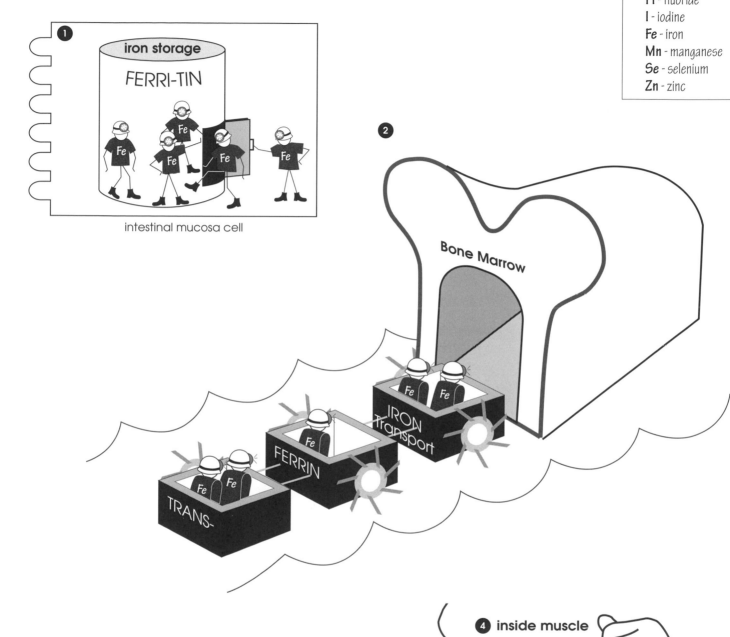

1 iron storage

FERRI-TIN

intestinal mucosa cell

2 Bone Marrow

IRON Transport

FERRIN

TRANS-

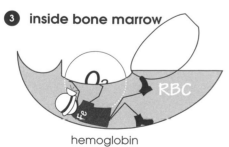

3 inside bone marrow

RBC

hemoglobin

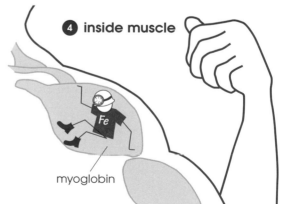

4 inside muscle

myoglobin

179

Trace Minerals:
Zinc

Minerals

Cu - copper
Cr - chromium
Fl - fluoride
I - iodine
Fe - iron
Mn - manganese
Se - selenium
Zn - zinc

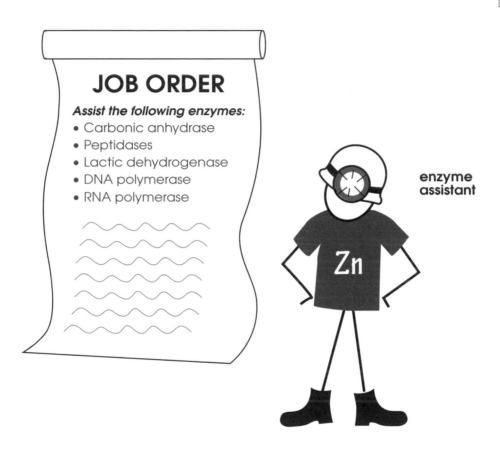

JOB ORDER

Assist the following enzymes:
- Carbonic anhydrase
- Peptidases
- Lactic dehydrogenase
- DNA polymerase
- RNA polymerase

enzyme assistant

The roles of protein include immune function, hormone construction and function, enzyme manufacture, and blood clotting. These all require the trace mineral zinc.

Zinc, in fact, is an assistant to several enzymes. Zinc assists enzymes that make the genetic material DNA and RNA. Enzymes in which chemical reactions involve carbon dioxide, enzymes involved in fat metabolism, and digestive enzymes all require zinc.

Like iron, zinc is handled by both transfer and storage proteins. Several body functions would be impaired without this important trace mineral. Animal protein provides zinc in the diet.

Trace Minerals:
Iodine

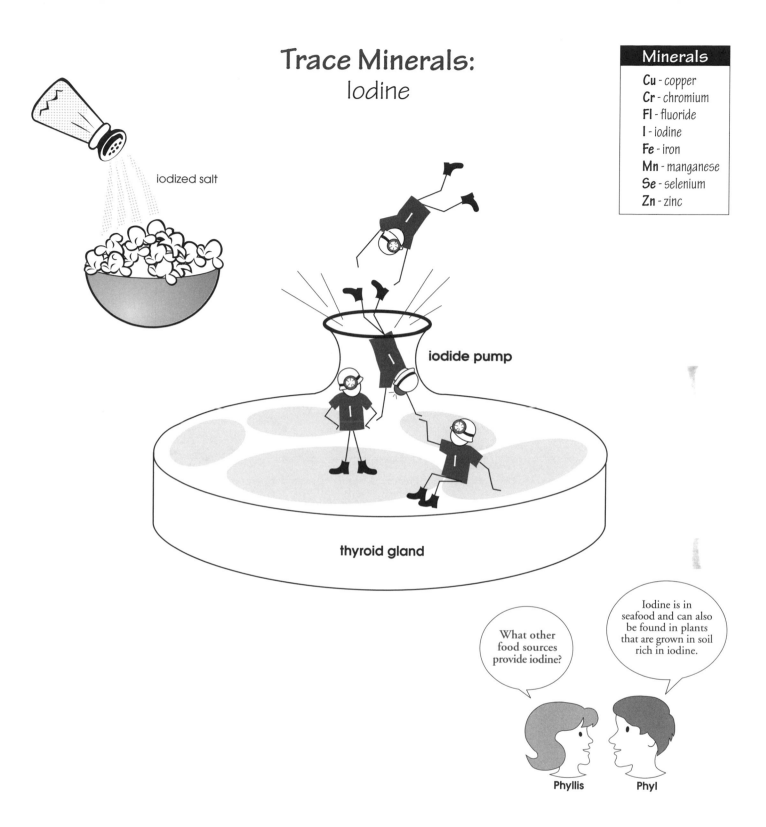

Minerals
Cu - copper
Cr - chromium
Fl - fluoride
I - iodine
Fe - iron
Mn - manganese
Se - selenium
Zn - zinc

iodized salt

iodide pump

thyroid gland

What other food sources provide iodine?

Iodine is in seafood and can also be found in plants that are grown in soil rich in iodine.

Phyllis   Phyl

The iodized salt we sprinkle on foods provides the necessary iodine in the diet. Iodine is converted to the ion iodide in the digestive process.

Iodide ions are captured by a special pump and brought into the cells of the thyroid gland. Iodine is a major component of thyroid hormone secreted by this gland. Thyroid hormone regulates the metabolic rate of every cell in the human body. Stated simply, the metabolic rate is the rate at which cells use oxygen to make energy from nutrients. ATP is made from nutrients to fuel the functions of cells.

Trace Minerals:
Copper, Fluoride, Chromium, Selenium

The trace minerals copper and fluoride are found in drinking water. Copper helps make hemoglobin in red blood cells and the collagen for all of our tissues. Fluoride helps to prevent the bacterial process of tooth decay. It promotes the perfect formation of hydroxyapatite crystals in bones and teeth and may protect bones against fractures.

Chromium and selenium are found in meats, nuts, and whole grains. Chromium works along with the hormone insulin to help bring glucose molecules into cells. Selenium is part of the enzyme that works with vitamin E as an antioxidant to protect tissue structure.

Trace Minerals:
Importance in the Active Body

Minerals

Cu - copper
Cr - chromium
Fl - fluoride
I - iodine
Fe - iron
Mn - manganese
Se - selenium
Zn - zinc

Other trace minerals, such as molybdenum, nickel, and silicon, also occur in foods and participate in various functions and processes. Though we need only minuscule amounts of trace minerals, we could not exercise without them. We could not deliver oxygen to or transport carbon dioxide from working muscles. We could not bring glucose into muscle cells. Therefore we could not make enough ATP to do muscular work. We could not build protein for healthy muscle tissue to move the skeleton. The strength of the bones that make up our skeleton would be compromised. The teeth with which we chew foods to provide nutrients would likely decay. We could not digest foods properly to obtain their nutrients. Without the trace minerals our health would be severely impaired.

What is the function of bone?
How does bone change over time?

Bone is a latticework of fibrous connective tissue comprised principally of collagen. Bone is densely packed with crystals made of a mixture of calcium and phosphorus. The mixture is called hydroxyapatite.

There are two kinds of bone tissue. The more porous trabecular bone makes up the inner structure. The more solid cortical bone makes up the outer shell. Each bone in the body contains a different proportion of each kind of bone tissue.

As a dynamic and living tissue, bone is continuously remodeled. It is always breaking down and building up. Several factors at different stages of human development influence the remodeling. These factors include heredity, the actions of various hormones, and diet. Bone remodeling is influenced by biomechanical forces or stress. The anti-gravity work of resistance exercise also has an important effect on bone remodeling.

During childhood, the bone-building processes exceed the breakdown processes and bones grow in length, width, size, and mineral density. During adolescence, sex hormones cause rapid bone growth and development. In adulthood, at about age thirty, bone mass reaches its peak. A slow decline in bone density takes place between ages thirty-five and fifty. A rapid decline in bone density occurs around perimenopause and for about ten years after menopause.

During the remodeling processes, bones are broken down and rebuilt. The breakdown of bone is called resorption. Resorption occurs when bone cells called osteoclasts are activated and directed to dissolve and remove older bone matrix. During the rebuilding and mineralization process, bone-building cells called osteoblasts are activated and instructed to create new bone matrix.

Hydroxyapatite crystals are then packed into the formation sites where old bone matrix was removed. The density, and therefore strength, of bone is maintained during the remodeling process as long as the resorption site is entirely refilled with new materials. Bone density is lost if the site is not entirely refilled. Sometimes osteoclasts dissolve a cavity so large that osteoblasts do not refill it sufficiently. Sometimes osteoblasts simply do not make enough new bone. This may occur if an individual takes particular medications. Physicians should therefore advise patients when prescribing medications that may affect bone health. When the rate of bone loss exceeds that of new bone formation, the result is low bone mass. The structure of bone becomes weakened and its mechanical strength is compromised.

Low bone mass is also referred to as osteopenia. With osteopenia, the reduced density of bone structure increases one's risk of fracture. If the bone loss is not halted, or slowed, then further loss in structural integrity results in osteoporosis. Osteoporosis is a loss of bone mass that weakens the overall architecture of a given bone and significantly increases its risk of fracture.

Peak bone mass is attained when bone reaches its highest level of structural density. Bone mass reaches its peak in human males and females at around thirty years old. Men generally have a higher peak bone mass than women at age thirty.

Women lose less than one percent of their peak bone mass each year until the onset of menopause, at which time significant and increased bone loss occurs. The bone loss is particularly rapid during the first two years after menopause and then steadily declines for about ten years. Loss of bone mineral density in males occurs throughout life in a manner similar to that of women prior to menopause.

Low Bone Mass

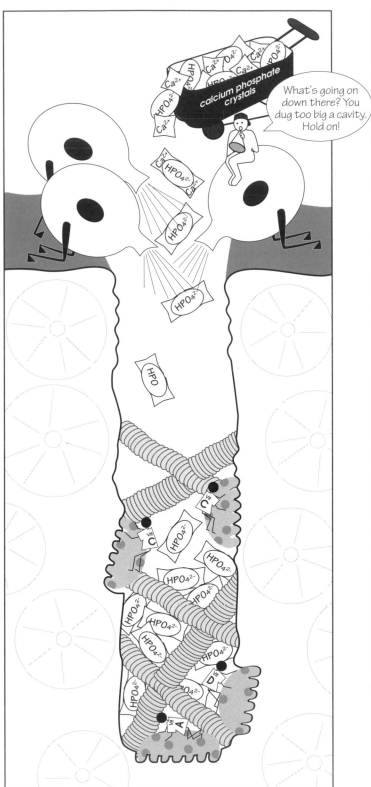

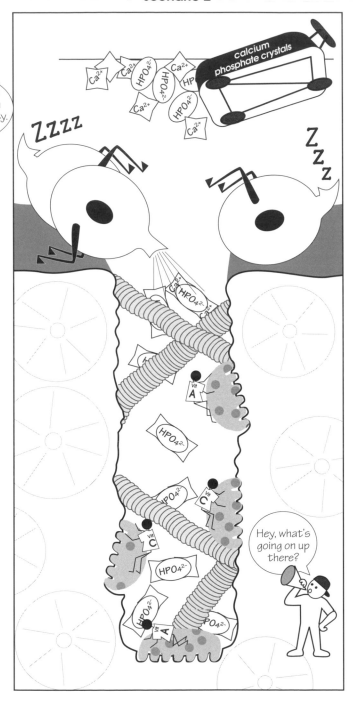

How is bone density measured?

The bone mineral density of the skeleton can be precisely and accurately measured with a technique called Dual Energy X-ray Aborptiometry (DEXA). A DEXA examination measures bone mineral content or density at specific sites. For example, it may be measured at the neck of the femur, where the thigh bone inserts into the hip joint, or at specific vertebrae of the spinal column. Bone mineral density is a direct measure of bone strength.

Available at many hospitals and clinics, this noninvasive procedure is crucial in the early detection of low bone density. Several measures can be taken to slow or minimize the loss of bone and rebuild new bone if discovered early.

Phyl and Phyllis's Physiology Phorum

Bone mineral density measurements are assessments of bone health. In 1994, guidelines were established by the World Health Organization in order to understand the value of bone mineral density levels. There are three categories of bone strength: normal, osteopenia (low bone mass), and osteoporosis.

Each category is a measure of the increasing risk of fracture. Osteoporosis is the diagnosis of highest risk. A diagnosis of osteoporosis means that the chance of getting fractures is greater than in an individual diagnosed as having osteopenia or normal bone mass.

Bone mineral density is a measure of the state of an individual's bone loss. There are other tests available that can also measure the rate of bone loss. These include urine and blood tests. The combination of these tests with a DEXA examination provides a dynamic view of bone change. This is especially important at times of rapid bone loss such as that which occurs in menopause. Knowing the rate of bone loss can be helpful in making decisions about preventive therapy.

While DEXA is regarded as the gold standard in the measurement of bone mineral density, there are other simple, noninvasive screening tests available. Heel ultrasound or wrist instruments may be used. Although they are not sensitive enough to be used as diagnostic tools, they do provide another method for assessing an individual's bone health.

How important is dietary calcium in maintaining bone mass?

Calcium is multifunctional. It is essential for nerve transmission, muscular contraction, blood clotting, and several other critical body functions. Blood calcium levels should therefore be carefully maintained and monitored. If dietary calcium is not adequate, calcium is removed from bone and pumped out into the blood.

Phyl and Phyllis's Physiology Phorum

It is especially important to obtain adequate calcium and vitamin D in the diet. It is best to obtain calcium in foods because constituents in these foods promote the absorption of calcium. Dairy products are notably rich in calcium. Other calcium-rich foods include salmon and such green leafy vegetables as spinach and broccoli. If the diet is low in calcium, dietary supplements such as calcium carbonate, calcium phosphate, and calcium citrate are recommended.

It is important to note that dietary calcium supplements are best absorbed in the body under particular circumstances. For example, it is recommended that calcium carbonate and calcium phosphate be taken with food. Digestive acids help them dissolve, which increases their overall absorption.

Calcium citrate can be taken on an empty stomach because it does not need an acidic environment to dissolve; it dissolves easily in water. Calcium supplements are best absorbed if they are consumed in small doses throughout the day with meals. Dosages should not exceed 500 mg at one meal.

Required Calcium

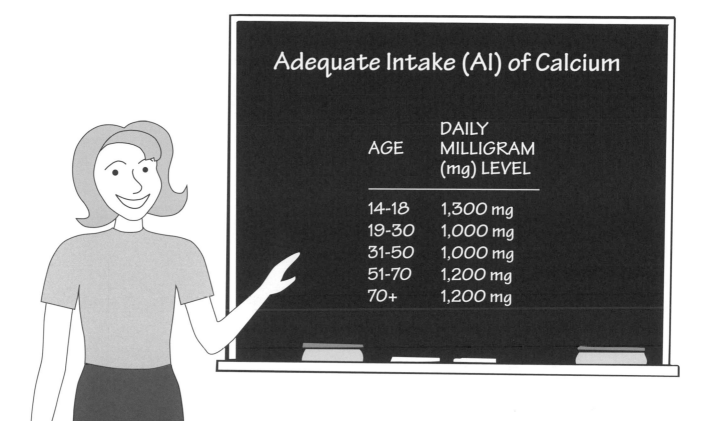

Adequate Intake (AI) of Calcium

AGE	DAILY MILLIGRAM (mg) LEVEL
14-18	1,300 mg
19-30	1,000 mg
31-50	1,000 mg
51-70	1,200 mg
70+	1,200 mg

Vitamin D is called a vitamin, but it is actually a hormone. An inactive form of vitamin D is converted to an active form through a complex process in the kidneys when the skin is exposed to the ultraviolet rays of sunlight.

Once activated, vitamin D helps to make the protein carrier that transports calcium into the bloodstream through the gastrointestinal tract. It also ensures that the kidneys retain calcium instead of excreting it in the urine. We can also obtain vitamin D in foods. It is added to several foods such as milk, fatty fish, butter, and cod liver oil.

It may be necessary to consult a nutritionist to determine individual calcium needs. However, there are recommendations established by the National Institutes of Health, the National Osteoporosis Foundation, the World Health Organization, and the Institute of Medicine. All of these organizations have websites that are listed in the bibliography and suggested reading.

189

What factors influence bone density?

There are a number of factors that influence bone density. In addition to several physiological factors, adequate dietary calcium, vitamin D, and physical activity also support maintenance of strong bones. Increased osteoblast activity and bone-building are stimulated by electrical currents. These occur as a result of the biomechanical forces or stress imposed on bones through impact, antigravity work or resistance exercise.

Resistance training, also known as strength training, is highly recommended, not only for maintenance of good posture and lean body mass but also for maintaining strong, dense bones. Whole body strength training programs should include resistance exercises that fatigue the major muscle groups of the body in eight to fifteen repetitions.

The female reproductive hormone, estrogen, also strongly influences bone density. Estrogen is used in reproductive tissue in the body during childbearing years. It influences many other tissues, including the walls of blood vessels, the brain, and bone.

Estrogen plays a particularly important role in the bone remodeling process. It influences the number and activity of the bone-building osteoblasts and enhances collagen production. Conversely, it decreases the activity of bone-dissolving osteoclasts. Estrogen therefore acts to prevent bone loss.

Encouraging Bone Production

Bone serves as an important reservoir, making calcium available for several important physiological functions. Blood calcium levels are carefully monitored and maintained by the actions of two hormones: parathyroid hormone and calcitonin. Parathyroid hormone (PTH) is manufactured and released by the parathyroid glands in response to low blood calcium levels. Parathyroid hormone acts directly in bone tissue to increase the bone-dissolving activity of osteoclasts. The calcium is then released into the bloodstream, making it available to other body tissues.

Calcitonin is produced and released by special cells of the thyroid gland. When the thyroid gland releases calcitonin, the result is the storage of calcium in bones. Calcitonin levels are raised by the hormone testosterone. Testosterone is primarily a male hormone, but it is also produced in the female adrenal gland in small amounts. Osteoblast activity and bone building are thus influenced both by calcitonin and testosterone as well as estrogen.

Factors Influencing Bone Density

Several factors interact to result in a gain, loss, or maintenance of bone density. When a woman ceases to menstruate, blood levels of estrogen are diminished, and the bone remodeling process is out of balance, resulting in a tendency toward bone loss. If this loss continues, bone mineral density decreases, and the risk for fracture increases. When this risk reaches a critical stage as measured by bone density tests, a woman may be diagnosed with post-menopausal osteoporosis.

Men may also develop osteoporosis. Their loss of bone, however, is more gradual. Generally, men at age thirty tend to have a higher peak bone mass than women. They also tend to lose bone later in life. Blood levels of the male hormone testosterone, which strongly influences BMD in men, diminish more gradually and later in life than do sex hormone levels in women. Thus a man's risk of osteoporosis occurs later in life.

What can be done to reduce bone loss?

The time to obtain a bone mineral density test is as close to menopause as possible. As previously discussed, a very rapid rate of bone loss is associated with the diminished hormone levels coincidental to menopause. This bone loss occurs for about ten years following menopause, primarily within the first two years after menopause begins.

Phyl and Phyllis's Physiology Phorum

Some women are quite lucky to have accumulated years of excellent bone density through active lifestyles and diet as well as strong heredity. For those women who are not as lucky, early detection of bone loss allows for immediate attention and appropriate preventive therapy. In addition to a calcium-rich diet and an exercise program that includes both weight-bearing cardiovascular activity and resistance training, sometimes drug therapy is recommended.

Different types of drugs are used, depending upon the needs of the individual. For post-menopausal women with symptoms, estrogen therapy is commonly recommended as an effective means of treating and slowing osteoporotic bone loss.

For those individuals who are not candidates for hormone replacement therapy, there are newly available medications for prevention of bone loss. These include FDA-approved medications such as raloxifene, alendronate, risedronate, salmon calcitonin, and teriparatide.

Phyl and Phyllis's
Physiology
Phorum

The FDA-approved drugs alendronate and risedronate are chemicals called bisphosphonates that are used to slow bone loss and increase bone mass. These drugs work to halt the osteoclastic resorption (excavation) process with the net result being an increase in BMD. The bisphosphonates have been very successful in long-term prevention of rapid bone loss.

Salmon calcitonin is available as nasal spray. While calcitonin inhibits osteoclast activity in bone and favors the bone-building process, it has been used for many years as an osteoporosis therapy with limited results.

Raloxifene is designed to work in bone and cardiovascular tissue and does not interact with breast or uterine tissue. It has been shown to slightly increase or maintain bone mineral density.

Teriparatide is the first bone-building medication to be used to treat osteoporosis. It works directly on the osteoblasts and increases their activity in

making new bone. Patients taking teriparatide have shown dramatic increases in bone mineral density and the medicine should prove to be extremely valuable, particularly for those individuals who have a history of fractures.

Along with any drug therapy for osteoporosis or osteopenia (low bone mass), it is essential to continue a diet adequate in calcium, regular anti-gravity cardiovascular activity, and progressive resistance training. This combination ensures the maintenance of adequate bone mass with the opportunity to build bone mass.

Though osteoporosis is not considered a life-threatening disease, a bone fracture can quickly alter the quality of life of any individual. Therefore, physicians are increasingly encouraging their patients to have baseline bone density measurements. Early detection, prevention, and elimination of risk factors are essential to maintain bone health.

Bibliography and Recommended Reading

American Alliance for Health, Physical Education, Recreation and Dance. *Physical Best Activity Guide: Middle and High School Levels, 2nd ed.* Champaign, Illinois: Human Kinetics, 2005.

American College of Sports Medicine. *Guidelines for Exercise Testing and Prescription, 7th ed.* Philadelphia, Pennsylvania: Lippincott, Williams & Wilkins, 2005.

American Diabetes Association. *Exchange Lists for Meal Planning.* Alexandria, Virginia: American Diabetes Association, 2003.

American Diabetes Association. *Handbook of Exercise in Diabetes.* Alexandria, Virginia: American Diabetes Association, 2002.

Antonio, J., and J. Scout. *Sports Supplements.* Philidelphia, Pennsylvania: Lippincott, Williams, & Wilkins, 2001.

Bar-Or, O., and T. W. Rowland. *Pediatric Exercise Medicine: from Physiologic Principles to Health Care Application.* Champaign, Illinois: Human Kinetics, 2004.

Bonnick, S. L. *Bone Densitometry in Clinical Practice, 2nd ed.* Totowa, New Jersey: Humana Press, 2004.

Bookspan, J. *Health & Fitness in Plain English, Updated Edition.* Monterrey, California: Healthy Learning, 2004.

Brown, W. H., C. S. Foote, and B. I. Iverson. *Organic Chemistry, 4th ed.* Belmont, California: Thomson Brooks, 2005.

Bryant, C., and B. Franklin. *Exercise Testing & Program Design: A Fitness Professional's Handbook.* Monterrey, California: Healthy Learning, 2002.

Bryant, C., and D. Green. *ACE Personal Trainer Manual: The Ultimate Resource for Fitness Professionals, 3rd ed.* San Diego, California: American Council on Exercise, 2003.

Carrico, M. *Fitness Yoga: A Guide for Fitness Professionals from the American Council on Exercise.* San Diego, California: Healthy Learning, 2005.

Centers for Disease Control and Prevention, Division of Nutrition and Physical Activity. *Promoting Physical Activity: A Guide for Community Action.* Champaign, Illinois: Human Kinetics, 1999.

Cooper, K. *FIT Kids! The Complete Shape-Up Program from Birth Through High School.* Nashville, TN: Broadman & Holman Publishers, 1999.

Cotton, R. C. *Clinical Exercise Specialist Manual: Ace's Source for Training Special Populations.* San Diego, California: American Council on Exercise, 1999.

Bibliography and Recommended Reading

Cotton, R. C. *Lifestyle and Weight Management Consultant Manual.* San Diego, California: American Council on Exercise, 1996.

Cotton, R. T., and D. Green. *Group Fitness Instructor Manual: ACE's Guide for Fitness Professionals, 1st ed.* San Diego, California: American Council on Exercise, 2000.

Delevier, F. *Strength Training Anatomy, 2nd ed.* Champaign, Illinois: Human Kinetics, 2006.

Faigenbaum, A., and W. Westcott. *Strength & Power for Young Athletes.* Champaign, Illinois: Human Kinetics, 2000.

Faigenbaum, A. and W. Westcott. *Youth Fitness.* San Diego, California: American Council on Exercise, 2001.

Girdano, D., D. Dusek, and G. Everly. *Controlling Stress and Tension, 7th ed.* Boston, Massachusetts: Pearson/Benjamin Cummungs, 2005.

Goodman, H. M. *Basic Medical Endocrinology, 3rd ed.* New York, New York: Academic Press, 2003.

Griffin, J. C. *Client-Centered Exercise Prescription, 2nd ed.* Champaign, Illinois: Human Kinetics, 2006.

Guyton, A., and J. Hall. *Textbook of Medical Physiology, 11th ed.* Philadelphia, Pennsylvania: Elsevier Saunders, 2006.

Headley, S., and S. Massad. *Nutritional Supplements For Athletes.* Reston, Virginia: AAHPERD Publications, 1999.

Heyward, V. *Advanced Fitness Assessment & Exercise Prescription, 4th ed.* Champaign, Illinois: Human Kinetics, 2002.

Howley, E. T. *Health Fitness Instructor's Handbook, 4th ed.* Champaign, Illinois: Human Kinetics, 2003.

Isaacs, L. D., and R. Pohlman. *Preparing for the ACSM Health/Fitness Instructor Certification Examination, 2nd ed.* Champaign, Illinois: Human Kinetics, 2004.

Kraemer, W., and S. Fleck. *Strength Training for Young Athletes, 2nd ed.* Champaign, Illinois: Human Kinetics, 2005.

Levy, M. *Power at the Plate: The Safe and Sensible Guide to Healthy Eating and Weight Control.* Northbrook, Illinois: Merle Levy, LNC, Inc., 2002.

McArdle W., F. Katch, and V. Katch. *Sports and Exercise Nutrition, 2nd ed.* Philadelphia, Pennsylvania: Lippincott, Williams & Wilkins, 2005.

Bibliography and Recommended Reading

McArdle, W., F. Katch, and V. Katch. *Exercise Physiology: Energy, Nutrition and Human Performance, 6th ed.* Philadephia, Pennsylvania: Lippincott, Williams & Wilkins, 2006.

McGill, S. *Low Back Disorders : Evidence-Based Prevention and Rehabilitation, 1st ed.* Champaign, Illinois: Human Kinetics, 2002.

Medical Economics Research Group. *The PDR Family Guide to Prescription Drugs, 7th ed.* New York, New York: Three Rivers Press, 1999.

Notelovitz M, D. Tonnessen, and S. Meek. *Stand Tall! Every Women's Guide to Preventing and Treating Osteoporosis 2nd ed.* Gainesville, Florida: Triad Publishing, 1998.

Orwoll, E. *Osteoporosis in Men: The Effects of Gender on Skeletal Health.* San Diego, California: Academic Press, 1999.

Porth, C. *Pathophysiology: Concepts of Altered Health States, 7th ed.* Philadelphia, Pennsylvania: Lippincott, Williams & Wilkins, 2005.

Powers S., and E. Howley. *Exercise Physiology: Theory and Application to Fitness and Performance, 6th ed.* Dubuque, Iowa: Maidenhead, McGraw-Hill Education, 2006.

Richmond, M. *Physiology Storybook: An Owner's Manual for the Human Body.* Northbrook, Illinois: JOIE Publications, 2000.

Sharkey, B. *Physiology of Fitness, 3rd ed.* Champaign, Illinois: Human Kinetics, 1990.

U.S. Department of Agriculture and U.S. Department of Health and Human Services. *Nutrition and Your Health: Dietary Guidelines for Americans, 5th ed.* Washington D.C.: U.S. Department of Human Services, Government Printing Office, 2000.

U.S. Department of Health and Human Services. *Healthy People 2010: Understanding and Improving Health.* Washington D.C.: U.S. Department of Health and Human Services, Government Printing Office, 2000.

United States Department of Agriculture. *Dietary Guidelines for Americans, 2005, 6th ed.* Washington, DC: United States Government, 2005.

Westcott, W., and T. D'Arpino. *High-Intensity Strength Training.* Champaign, Illinois: Human Kinetics, 2003.

Westcott, W. *Building Strength & Stamina, 2nd ed.* Champaign, Illinois: Human Kinetics, 2003.

Health and Fitness Web Sites

American Council on Exercise (ACE) .... www.acefitness.org

American College of Sports Medicine (ACSM) .... www.acsm.org

Aerobics and Fitness Association of American (AFAA) .... www.afaa.com

National Academy of Sports Medicine (NASM) .... www.nasm.org

American Alliance for Health, Physical Education,
Recreation and Dance (AAHPERD) .... www.aahperd.org

IDEA Health & Fitness Association (IDEA) .... www.ideafit.com

Institute of Medicine (IOM) .... www.iom.edu

The Cooper Institute .... www.cooperinst.org

American Heart Association .... www.americanheart.org

American Diabetes Association .... www.diabetes.org

United States Department of Agriculture (USDA) .... www.usda.gov

USDA Dietary Guidelines .... www.mypyramid.gov/guidelines

United States Department of Health and Human Services .... www.hhs.gov

National Institutes of Health .... www.nih.gov

National Osteoporosis Foundation (NOF) .... www.nof.org

Centers for Disease Control and Prevention .... www.cdc.gov

The President's Council on Physical Fitness and Sports .... www.fitness.gov

World Health Organization (WHO) .... www.who.org

National Diabetes Information Clearinghouse .... diabetes.niddk.nih.gov

Index

About the Author

Marla Richmond, an internationally recognized expert in exercise science, presents her exciting and innovative educational approach to physical and health educators, fitness and medical professionals, national and international organizations, schools, libraries and institutions of higher learning worldwide. She is a practicing exercise physiologist, health and lifestyle counselor and researcher.

In addition to The Physiology Storybook, Richmond is the author of The Art and Science of Getting Strong and Eating Right, a teen and family fitness guide that includes an original musical CD, published in cooperation with the American Council on Exercise.

Richmond writes "Fit Bits," a monthly wellness column for Pioneer Press newspapers serving several Chicago area communities, and the Northwestern University "Fit Bite," a monthly newsletter for the Evanston campus in Illinois. She also serves as an expert consultant on health and exercise for television, radio, magazines and newspapers. She is a frequent guest lecturer at medical and nursing schools.

Her Physiology Storybook projects have been supported by a number of organizations, including the American Council on Exercise, PBS Teachers Source, the National Association of Sport and Physical Education and the Medical Fitness Association.

She is a member of the American Physiological Society, the American College of Sports Medicine, the American Council on Exercise, the Medical Fitness Association, and the American Alliance for Health Education, Recreation, and Dance. She is also a member of the American Diabetes Association, and serves on advisory boards of fitness organizations throughout the world.

Pursuing her passion for the study of the human body, Richmond received her Master of Science degree in Exercise Physiology from Benedictine University in Lisle, Illinois. She received her bachelor's degree in communications, with an emphasis in public speaking, and a double minor in psychology and creative writing from the University of Arizona in Tucson. She also attended DePaul University in Chicago to study kinesiology and exercise physiology.

As a fitness and wellness professional, she promotes balance and healing and shares her knowledge through original creative illustrations and in plain, helpful language (with a touch of humor) to both the lay and medical community. She enjoys running, hiking, biking and a variety of other physical activities in addition to her teaching, speaking and writing. She resides in the Chicago area.